the land of Ireland

Brian de Breffny

photographs by George Mott

Abradale Press / Harry N. Abrams, Inc.
New York

Page 1: *A farmstead below Crotlieve, County Down, Ulster;* pages 2-3: *The Upper Lake, Glendalough, County Wicklow, Leinster;* pages 4-5: *Limestone boulder, the Burren, County Clare, Munster;* pages 6-7: *Joyce's River, Connemara, named for a Welsh family that settled in this remote region of County Galway, Connacht.*

Editor: Michael George
Designer: Gilda Kuhlman
Map Illustrations: Carol Ann Robson

Library of Congress Cataloging in Publication Data

De Breffny, Brian.
  The land of Ireland.

  Originally published: New York: H. N. Abrams, 1979.
  Bibliography: p. 241
  Includes index.
  1. Ireland—Description and travel—1951–1980.
2. Ireland—History. 3. Northern Ireland—Description
and travel. 4. Northern Ireland—History. I. Title.
DA978.D4 1985   941.5   84–16841
ISBN 0–8109–8066–5

Printed and bound in Japan

Acknowledgments

The author and the photographer wish to thank many friends in Ireland for their suggestions and encouragement, and in particular Sean Rafferty of B.B.C., Belfast for his help and hospitality and the staff of the Irish Georgian Society, Castletown, Celbridge for their many kindnesses. Nicola Boland typed the manuscript.

The author and photographer also wish to acknowledge the following for permission to quote:

Martin Brian and O'Keefe Ltd., and Katherine B. Kavanagh, for "Shancoduff" by Patrick Kavanagh; Spencer Curtis Brown and Longmans Ltd. for the passages from *Bowen's Court* by Elizabeth Bowen; Christine, Countess of Longford for "The Flight of the Earls," translated by the Sixth Earl of Longford; Dr. Maurice Craig for his "Ballad to a Traditional Refrain"; Dolmen Press and the respective poets for John Montague's versions of "The Muse of Amergin," "The Vikings," "Columcille," "The Hag of Beare," and "Liádan's Lament," for "King John's Castle" by Thomas Kinsella, for David Marcus' version of "The Midnight Court," and for "Echo at Coole" by Austin Clarke; Faber and Faber Ltd. for "Dublin Made Me" from *The Hungry Grass* by Donagh MacDonagh and for "The Hedgehog" from *New Weather* by Paul Muldoon; Faber and Faber Ltd. and Oxford University Press, Inc. for "Viking Dublin: Trial Pieces" from *North* by Seamus Heaney, copyright © 1969 by Seamus Heaney; Michael Hartnett and New Writer's Press for Michael Hartnett's version of "Marban, A Hermit Speaks"; the Dr. Douglas Hyde Trust for his "If I Were to Go West" from *Love Songs of Connacht*; John V. Kelleher for his version of "Cú Chuimne in Youth"; the estate of the late Donagh MacDonagh for his "A Warning to Conquerors"; Macmillan Publishing Co., Inc. for "Under Ben Bulben" from *The Collected Poems of W.B. Yeats* by William Butler Yeats, copyright 1940 by Georgie Yeats, renewed 1968 by Bertha Georgie Yeats, Michael Butler Yeats, and Anne Yeats, for "Coole Park, 1929" and "In Memory of Eva Gore-Booth and Con Markiewicz" from *The Collected Poems of W.B. Yeats* by William Butler Yeats, copyright 1933 by Macmillan Publishing Co., Inc., renewed 1961 by Bertha Georgie Yeats, for "The Tower" and "My House" from *The Collected Poems of W.B. Yeats* by William Butler Yeats, copyright 1928 by Macmillan Publishing Co., Inc., renewed 1956 by Georgie Yeats, for "The Wild Swans at Coole" from *The Collected Poems of W.B. Yeats* by William Butler Yeats, copyright 1919 by Macmillan Publishing Co., Inc., renewed 1947 by Bertha Georgie Yeats, for "The Lake Isle of Innisfree" from *The Collected Poems of W.B. Yeats* by William Butler Yeats, copyright 1906 by Macmillan Publishing Co., Inc., renewed 1934 by W.B. Yeats; Oxford University Press for Robin Flower's translation of "This Night Sees Ireland Desolate" from *The Irish Tradition* by Robin Flower, copyright 1947 by Oxford University Press, for the poems by J.M. Synge from *The Collected Works of J.M. Synge,* Vol. I *Poems,* edited by Robin Skelton, copyright 1962 by Oxford University Press; James Simmons for his version of "A Hermit's Song"; Arland Ussher for his translation of "The Midnight Court"; Miss Anne Yeats and M.B. Yeats for the seven poems by William Butler Yeats from *The Collected Poems of W.B. Yeats* by William Butler Yeats.

Contents

Introduction

"Lord, how quickly doth that country alter one's nature," wrote the Elizabethan poet Edmund Spenser, whose years as a colonist in Ireland left him with a love for the land but no love for the Irish. For centuries before the time of Spenser and the Elizabethan adventurers who sought to colonize Ireland, and since, the country has attracted, fascinated, and captivated strangers, who often became more Irish than the Irish, and has forever held the indigenous Irish themselves in its thrall.

That appeal is in the mountains, at the seashore, beside the many tranquil lakes, the bright rivers, and the sleepy canals, in the lovely gardens and old demesnes, and in the lush water meadows, in the shade of creeper-clad ruined castles, in the brilliant hedgerows of fuchsia and of whitethorn, and on the rough lonely islands of the West. The words of the toast in which one Irishman wishes another the happiness of "death in Ireland" have a token of that fierce, sweet attachment of the Irish to their land, their passionate and obsessive love for a country which, in the past, has yielded so much hardship and bitterness, and repaid their loyalty with hunger and distress. So great has this love been that those Irish who sought new homes in distant countries passed it on to their children, and it survives among their descendants in the Irish diaspora.

Ireland was already famous for its lush vegetation two thousand years ago when the first Roman geographer, Pomponius Mela, a contemporary of Christ and a native of Spain, wrote his *De Situ Orbis* (Description of the World). He drew mainly on the earlier works of Greek geographers but he was more familiar with Western Europe than they had been, and although he may never have visited Ireland himself, he was able to report that while its climate was unfavorable for the ripening of grain, the herbage was so luxurious and savory, its quality so nutritious, that the cattle ate their fill early in the day, and if they were not restrained from feeding, they would, by eating too long, burst.

Ireland is still largely a pastoral country today, as it has been for centuries, and famed for its fine fat cattle and rich dairy products. The superficial appearance of the land has changed, however, since the Middle Ages, due to the clearance of the forests, and the plantations of the sixteenth and seventeenth centuries, when a determined effort was made to colonize and anglicize the rural areas and to create new urban nuclei. The unbaptized beauty of the earlier Ireland is extolled in the *Leabhar Gabhala* (The Book of Invasions), a mythopoetic account of the arrival of the first inhabitants, in which the muse of Amergin, the chief bard of the Milesians and reputedly the first poet of Ireland, declares:

I speak for Erin,
Sailed and fertile sea,
Fertile fruitful mountains,
Fruitful moist woods,
Moist overflowing lochs,
Flowing hillside springs...

The fertile sea of Amergin's muse, the mountains, the moist woods, the numerous lakes, and the hillside springs still enchant the inhabitant and the visitor. Ireland has managed to retain much of its quite mystical beauty despite man's depredations of eight thousand years and despite the encroachments of a modern industrial society over the last fifty years. So sensitive to the charm of the land was the saintly Columcille, who lived in the sixth century, that he admitted to loving the land of Ireland almost beyond speech. Many ascetic monks of the early Irish church, recognizing that their love for Ireland was so close to physical love, felt a penitential need to exile themselves from their lovely island. This strong feeling of attachment persists. In this century it has been beautifully expressed by the great Irish poet, Patrick Kavanagh, in a poignant description of an old farmer who had "made a field his bride." Notwithstanding the challenge of urban consumerism, which questions belief in the authenticity of rural life, the Irish way of life is still intimately related to the land, as it has been time out of mind.

Irish legend preserves the account of Saint Brendan's voyage to the American continent in the sixth century in a leather boat. Intrepid twentieth-century sailors have now proved that such an exploit was indeed possible and could, therefore, have occurred. However, until only five hundred years ago, the Atlantic coast of Ireland was for all practical purposes the western extremity of the known world.

Going about Ireland today it is still not difficult to conjure visions of the pagan world before Patrick's time; the ancient standing stones and stone circles evoke its ceremonies, its games, its feasts and dances. Few landscapes in the world can be more instinct with myth and history. So much remains of the past: the burial places of prehistoric man, the forts, the monuments, the mines of the Bronze Age and the Iron Age, the early homesteads, the raths, the crannogs (artificial islets in the lakes or swamps where dwellings were built for safety from marauders and predators), the beehive-shaped stone cells, the little stone chapels and the intricately carved High Crosses of the monks of the Celtic Christian Church which flourished when barbarians overran most of Europe, the coastal towns founded by the invading Vikings from Scandinavia and the tall, slender, Round Towers which guarded the ecclesiastical settlements in those troubled times, the earthworks and the ruined castles and abbeys built by the invading Normans, the ubiquitous tower houses of the medieval magnates who lived precariously among an alien people, the town walls breached by the ruthless Cromwellian troops, the tree-lined avenues and demesne walls which are often all that remain of the carefully planted parks of the new aristocracy, grandiose piers of the gateway to a vanished mansion, neglected mills built during the boom when Ireland provided food for the British troops who fought Napoleon, abandoned stone cottages and crumbling cabins of the wretched people who fled the Famine and the land they loved. Beyond the lush meadow lands and the fields green with oats or barley, and the white hawthorn flowers in the hedgerows, there lie, in the words of the poet Donagh MacDonagh, the "raw and hungry hills of the West, the lean road flung over profitless bog, where only a snipe could rest." Over the centuries the people learned to bear the terrible hardship of those raw lands with characteristic fortitude and often reckless gaiety.

Although, politically and culturally, Ireland is becoming daily more involved with the rest of Europe, geographically it remains an Atlantic outpost, an island where maritime influences condition the climate and the land. The fame of rain in Ireland is perhaps as great as that of the greenness of much of the countryside. In fact, the rainfall is not excessive in quantity; it ranges from 140 centimeters annually in the Southwest to 70 centimeters in the East. It is the number of days each year on which rain actually falls that is high. The temperature is rarely high, even in the summer months; in the cloudy West primroses and wood sorrel thrive on treeless hillsides, whereas they normally grow only in shady dells and woods. The rapid changes in wind and cloud make for endless gradations of light.

Geologists have ascertained that the oldest known rocks in Ireland, at Kilmore Quay and Rosslare, in the southeastern county of Wexford, date from the pre-Cambrian era, two thousand million years ago. In the Paleozoic and Mesozoic eras vast upheavals of the landmass occurred. Then, in the Tertiary period of the Cenozoic era, almost the entire land was buried under an extensive covering of ice. Fluctuating warm and cold periods followed. Ten million years ago, when some of the dominant features of Ireland's rocky skeleton were formed, the country was densely wooded with warmth-demanding trees, but a subsequent cold period destroyed this exotic vegetation. About two million years ago there was a long period of intense cold with temperatures below freezing point. The actual relief of the modern landscape dates largely from the profound changes that took place in the Quaternary period about one-and-a-half million years ago, when postglacial erosion radically altered the scenery.

Until at least ten thousand years ago, and perhaps until as recently as seven or eight thousand years ago, Ireland was linked by land bridges to Britain. Before Ireland became an island, animals and plants immigrated. The giant deer that roamed Europe, North Africa, and North Asia twelve thousand years ago, reached Ireland. The male was a magnificent creature, about two meters high at its shoulders. It needed a large supply of calcium-rich vegetable matter to regrow its antlers, which reached a span of three meters before their annual shedding. Not all the continental land mammals that reached Britain crossed over into Ireland before the land bridges were submerged, and slow-moving reptiles never made it at all. The shortfall in plant immigration is even more noticeable; about half the flowering plants, ferns, and mosses that reached Britain, among them the small-leaved lime tree, the field maple, and the hornbeam, failed to reach Ireland. The beech tree, which now thrives in favorable climatic conditions in Ireland, was imported only in the eighteenth century to embellish the newly laid-out demesnes. The first trees to arrive with the milder climate and the return of the flora and fauna ten thousand years ago were the juniper and the willow, soon outstripped and supplanted by the birch, which flourished, but was in turn outstripped by the next arrivals about nine thousand years ago, the hazel and the pine. Oak, elm, and elder also arrived before the end of the immigratory period, but hazel led the field in growth and quantity for several thousand years. Pondweeds, bulrushes, water lilies, and sedge grew in the great lowland lakes before the formation of the fens and bogs; as the accumulation of vegetable debris surpassed its rate of decay, the bogs grew up. Peat, rich in sedge, willow, and birch debris, was formed on the margins of the lakes and rivers. Consequently the lakes shrank in size and the encroaching bog began to engulf the great primeval forest.

The next onslaught on the forest came from man, who first appeared in Ireland about the same time as the land bridges disappeared. The first known inhabitants: hunters, fowlers, and fishers who used flint instruments, appear to have left again or died out after their hunting forays. Next came a seminomadic people, also hunters, fowlers, and fishers with no agricultural skills, who frequented the coastal region or the shores of lakes and rivers. Radiocarbon tests give a date of 8,150 years ago on charcoal vestiges of their earliest known habitat, and of 7,500 years ago at a coastal site. The settlements in the northeastern part of the country would seem to indicate that these people came across from the coast of Scotland and perhaps originally from Scandinavia or some other part of northwestern Europe. Examination of the sites inhabited by these primitive people indicate that their diet included shellfish—limpets and oysters; fish, which they ate both smoked and dried; hazelnuts; and water-lily seeds. Living in isolation on the island they appear to have made no technical or cultural progress for two or three thousand years until the arrival of the next distinct wave of immigrants. Neolithic farming people arrived in Ireland when it was already surrounded by sea, 5,500 years ago. Within about one thousand years of their arrival these immigrants had spread across the island. They appear to have been of Mediterranean origin, having come from what is now Spain and Portugal, moving northward along the Atlantic coast of France through Brittany. In Ireland, the stone monuments they constructed, burial places and shrines, have survived, impressive reminders on the landscape of their civilization and of megalithic art. Dr.

Michael Herity, the archeologist, has calculated that one million man-days of labor were required to build Newgrange, their most impressive achievement.

The Beaker Folk, so named for the pottery vessels that they made and used, spread westward across Europe, reaching Ireland about 2000 B.C. The considerable quantity of their pottery that has been found in Ireland indicates that these immigrants were numerous and that they must be among the progenitors of the modern Irish population, for it is reasonable to conclude that they and the earlier agrarian settlers were assimilated by more sophisticated later immigrants, the Bronze Age metalworkers and the Celts.

The use of metal in the Bronze Age brought prospectors to Ireland where their search was rewarded by finds of metal ores and alluvial gold. By the eighth century B.C. the metalworkers were manufacturing bronze buckets, cauldrons, shields, and even trumpets. The goldsmiths also attained a high standard of workmanship in the ornaments that they made. At that time there was considerable population growth and, with the introduction of the plow in a primitive form, technological advancement. It was about that time, too, that the inhabitants began to build hill forts.

It appears that the first Celts may have arrived toward the end of the Bronze Age; certainly in the Iron Age, which followed, there is evidence of their establishment in Ireland and it may be inferred that they arrived before, and most probably well before, the first century A.D. when the Romans invaded and occupied neighboring Britain, for the Roman historians made no mention of the invasion of Ireland by the Celts. Stone and gold articles have been found in Ireland, exquisitely decorated in the Celtic La Tène style, which flourished in Continental Europe between the fifth and first centuries B.C. It is reasonable, therefore, to date the arrival of the Celts to about 300 B.C., a time at which there is evidence of a renewal of agricultural activity in the country. The Celtic warriors, who came with their refined artifacts and superior technology, were able to subdue and acculture the earlier inhabitants, so that the civilization that developed in Ireland, although it must have embraced a large non-Celtic population, was Celtic in its linguistic, legal, and social structures.

Many thousands of raths mark the Irish landscape. These circular plots, surrounded by a bank of earth and a ditch to protect the enclosure from human marauders and animal predators, were the homesteads of Celtic society.

Within the safety of such compounds, commonly called ring forts, ritual ceremonies like the inauguration of the pagan priest-kings on the Hill of Tara were performed.

By the seventh century A.D., when Celtic Ireland had become Christian, the country was divided into about one hundred and fifty petty kingdoms called *tuatha*. Powerful rulers built up an ascendancy of a group of these *tuatha* but respected their autonomy regarding their internal administration and jurisdiction. By the twelfth century, prior to the arrival of the Normans from England, there were about thirty of these larger ascendant units or kingdoms in the country. Ulster, Leinster, Munster and Connacht emerged as the four greatest kingdoms, and in time, swallowing the Kingdom of Meath, and with some boundary changes, these became the four provinces of Ireland to each of which an essay in this book is devoted.

In the first millennium of our era the Munstermen fought the men of Ulster and the men of Connacht raided the lands of Leinster, while within the major kingdoms themselves there were interminable feuds and internecine struggles. Today, the Munstermen, the Leinstermen, the men of Connacht, and some of the Ulstermen are united as citizens of the Republic of Ireland, which achieved independence from the British Crown in 1922, seven hundred and fifty years after Henry II's invasion of the country, while the people of six of the counties of the province of Ulster remain politically attached to the United Kingdom. The individual identity of each province and its people has not, however, disappeared. In some manner and measure each has retained its own personality, and even though the island is small in size, each province does differ in landscape and to some degree in climate. Unmistakably different accents and modes of speech have survived in both the Irish and English languages, as well as differences in customs, physical traits, and traits of character. Successive incomers to the country have woven a cultural fabric of many strands in Ireland, and according to their numbers and the areas of their settlement, this fabric is noticeably different in each province.

Ireland's history has in varying degrees left its stamp: at first the prehistoric inhabitants, then the Celts, and the flourishing Paleo-Christian Church; the three hundred years of medieval Viking history in Ireland, the colonial and military enterprises of the Anglo-Normans, and the establishment of the Pale of Settlement in Leinster; the gallowglass mercenaries who came and settled, the Tudor plantation schemes which brought English adventurers and yeoman farmers in the sixteenth century, the confiscation of monastic property, the Plantation of Ulster with the settlement of numerous Scots and the foundation of towns, the insurrection of 1641; the Cromwellian program of settlement and resettlement in the seventeenth century, the industrious Quaker and Huguenot incomers, merchants and artisans, the Dutch and the Palatines, the exodus of thousands of Jacobites to the Continent; the affluence of the great landlords in the eighteenth century and their taste for grandeur, accompanied by the reemergence of the Irish craftsman-designer, and the laying-out of many small rural towns and villages; the Penal Laws which restricted the ownership of land, the Rising of 1798, the Act of Union of 1800 with the demise of the Dublin Parliament, then Roman Catholic emancipation and the emergence of ultramontane Catholic triumphalism in the last century; the Famine in the 1840s with the consequent depopulation due to death and decades of emigration, the industrialization of Ulster and its relative prosperity in the late Victorian era; agrarian unrest, the Land Act of 1903 and the consequent redistribution of the land in this century followed by the disappearance of the majority of the Anglo-Irish landed gentry and the "Big House"; the struggle for independence, the Civil War, the division of the country in 1922, the growth of industry in the Republic, the guerrilla activities of the Irish Republican Army and the Provisionals in the last decade, and most recently of all, the entry of Ireland into the European Economic Community.

It is possible to say of Ireland, as Saki wrote of Crete, that it is a country that has made more history than it could consume.

Perched atop the cliffs of Moher, County Clare, Munster, O'Brien's Tower was built by Cornelius O'Brien, a local magnate, in 1835.

18

opposite: *Rhododendrons, the gardens of Howth Castle, County Dublin, Leinster.*

above: *"Giant's Eye," Giant's Causeway, County Antrim, Ulster.*

below: *Rock formation, Skelpoonagh Bay, near Glencolumbkille, County Donegal, Ulster.*

Ulster

*"Along the rough
and crooked lane"*

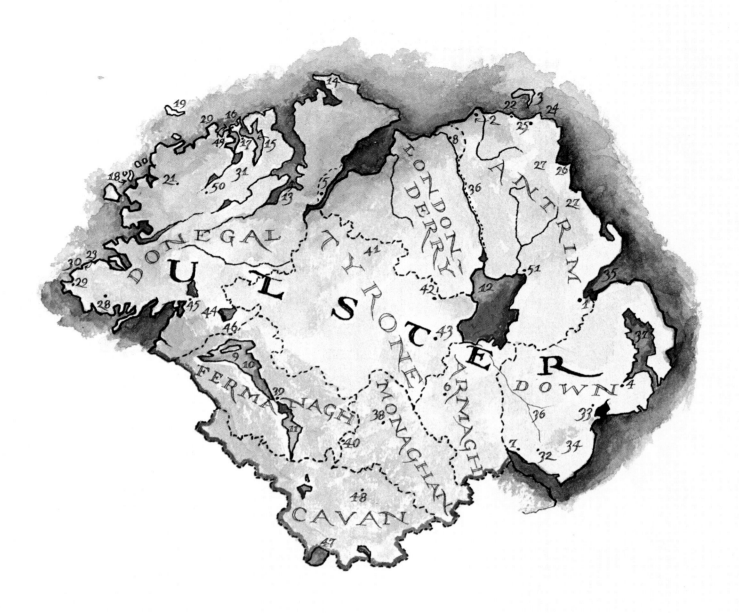

1	Belfast	18	Cruit Island	35	Belfast Lough
2	Giant's Causeway	19	Tory Island	36	River Bann
3	Rathlin Island	20	Horn Head	37	Strangford Lough
4	Downpatrick	21	Gweedore	38	Monaghan
5	Londonderry (Derry)	22	Dunluce Castle	39	Enniskillen
6	Armagh	23	Glen Head	40	Clones
7	Narrow Water	24	Fair Head	41	Sperrin Mountains
8	Coleraine	25	Ballycastle	42	Cookstown
9	Boa Island	26	Garron Point	43	Dungannon
10	Lower Lough Erne	27	Glens of Antrim	44	Lough Derg
11	Upper Lough Erne	28	Carrick	45	Donegal
12	Lough Neagh	29	Glencolumbkille	46	Pettigo
13	Lough Swilly	30	Skelpoonagh Bay	47	Lough Sheelin
14	Malin Head	31	Rock of Doon	48	Quilca
15	Mulroy Bay	32	Crotlieve	49	Doagh
16	Rosguill Peninsula	33	Dundrum	50	Glenveagh
17	Rosapenna	34	Mourne Mountains	51	Antrim

preceding spread: *A distant view of Downpatrick Cathedral,
County Down, supposed burial place of Saint Patrick.*

To many people the name of Ulster is identified with trouble. To those who love the province its name evokes the beautiful mountains of the ancient kingdom of Mourne, the tranquil islet-dotted lakes of Fermanagh, the slow-rolling clouds over the wild landscape of Gweedore, the fruit-laden orchards of Armagh, the falls of peaty water cascading into topaz-colored pools in the mossy Antrim glens, the majestic cliffs of Rathlin Island, the haunt of seal, buzzard, puffin, guillemot, cormorant, and shag. But to outsiders the mere mention of Ulster conjures dark images of mean, bomb-scarred city streets, of a bitter land where the evils of unemployment and sectarian strife fester.

Even in Ireland, Ulster often signifies only that northeastern part of the island which is still politically attached to Britain. In fact, the province of Ulster is itself divided by the same political boundary that divides the island. Only six of the nine counties of Ulster—Antrim, Armagh, Derry, Down, Fermanagh and Tyrone—are in the United Kingdom; the other three—Cavan, Donegal and Monaghan—are in the Republic of Ireland. Sometimes the border capriciously divides a farmer's land. The village of Pettigo has an Irish post office with a green letter box and a green telephone booth on one side of the main street, and on the other, a British post office with a red letter box and a red telephone booth. The people at one end of the street hold the green passports of the Republic of Ireland, their neighbors at the other end, subjects of the Queen of England, hold the blue British passports.

For one night, December 6, 1922, there existed an Irish Free State comprising the whole country. Why a political compromise split the province of Ulster and the land of Ireland cannot be easily explained. The reasons for the northern provincial parliament's voting out of the Irish Free State lie deeply embedded not only in centuries of Irish and British political and social history, but also in the history of the Reformation and the Counter-Reformation, with the cultural attitudes and societal patterns that they engendered, as well as in bygone European international dynastic intrigues, and in geographical factors which isolated parts of Ulster from the rest, and most of Ulster from the southern part of the country, so that it could survive longer as a Gaelic stronghold, behind its natural barriers.

It could be claimed that Irish history begins in Ulster, for the earliest reliable evidence of man's presence on the island about 6500 B.C. was found on Mount Sandel, south of Coleraine, in County Derry, and further early evidence was also found in Ulster, on the northwestern shore of Lough Neagh, the nearby banks of the Bann, and farther east along the coast of County Antrim, at Cushendun and at Larne, whence "Larnians," the name given to these people who lived a seminomadic life, fishing, trapping eel, and hunting waterfowl. Where the mesolithic Mount Sandelites and the Larnians came from is not known, but their settlement in northeastern Ireland suggests that they followed the route taken by many later immigrants across the narrow channel from the southwest of Scotland. The Larnians erected waterside dwellings, huts made of wattles, from the seventh to the fourth millennium B.C.

Between about 3500 and 3000 B.C. the Larnians were joined by newcomers, also of unknown racial origin, pioneer neolithic farmers who came first to the Ulster uplands, where they made clearings in the primeval forest to establish their agricultural settlements. It appears that advance parties must have come to scout the land, report on conditions, and study the tides and currents to facilitate the arduous and perilous task of transporting over the sea in skin boats whole families, together with domestic animals for husbandry, both breeding and milking, and a sufficient quantity of seed for their first crops. In clearing the forests, the first farmers made lasting changes to the landscape: first in Ulster, then elsewhere, as these people cleared then abandoned their agricultural patches, vast areas of hazel scrub grew in place of the original forest.

Once they had cleared a glade with their axes of flint, a material which was particularly abundant in Antrim, the primitive farmers erected a stockade as a protection against marauders and animal predators such as the wolf (which only died out in Ireland about two centuries ago), the boar, and the lynx. The foundations of one of their dwellings, roughly square in plan, about 6½ meters by 6, built of radially split oak planks, were discovered in 1967 on the crown of a low hill at Ballynagilly, near Cookstown, in County Tyrone. A carbon-14 test dated the vestiges of the timber house to between 3265 and 3165 B.C. At Ringneill Quay on Strangford Lough, in County Down, the earliest remains in Ireland of domestic animals, bones of ox, pig, and goat or possibly sheep, were discovered and dated by radiocarbon testing to within about one hundred years of the Ballynagilly house. Ballynagilly is the earliest neolithic settlement so far discovered in Ireland, charcoal from a pit on the site being about four to five hundred years older than the house. Flint arrowheads and pottery shards were also excavated on the site. Pottery remains of the neolithic period have been found in great numbers on numerous sites, while in one pit alone at Larne Harbour, County

Antrim, fifteen thousand pieces of worked flint were found. A rock called Porcellanite, outcrops of which occur at Tievebulliagh, County Antrim, and on Rathlin Island off the north coast of Antrim, was used to manufacture axes which were exported from these "factories." They have been found in many parts of Scotland and even in the south of England.

One of the earliest megalithic monuments in Ulster was found at Ballymacdermot, County Armagh. It is a communal burial place of the type known as the court grave, of which about three hundred have so far been discovered in Ireland, exclusively in Ulster and in northern Connacht. A segmented gallery consisting of stone chambers where the burials took place was fronted by a roofless semicircular or half-oval court, which appears to have been used for the rites. The Ballymacdermot court grave was constructed about 2800 B.C. Another, at Ballymacaldrack, County Antrim, known as Doey's Cairn, can be dated to the same epoch. At Cohaw in County Cavan and at Ballywholan in County Tyrone, are examples of double court graves constructed back to back in the same cairn with a court at each end. Near Glencolumbkille in County Donegal, at Malinmore (Cloghanmore) and Farranmacbride (Mannernamortee), are double court graves constructed so that the two courts form a central oval arena.

Portal graves, simple megalithic tombs consisting of a massive capstone raised with considerable technical skill onto standing stone pillars and usually erected on low ground, frequently near water, were a later development of the court grave builders. They are found more frequently in Ulster than in the rest of the island. The most graceful and impressive example is at Legananny on the slope of Crotlieve Mountain in County Down. Others in the same county are situated at Kilfeaghan, where the capstone is estimated to weigh forty tons, and at Goward near Hilltown, where there is an even more impressive one, long known as Finn McCool's Fingerstone after a legendary giant who is supposed to have thrown it there and left his finger marks on the stone; it is now called "Pat Kearney's Big Stone." Another portal grave in County Down, at Ballynahatten, was removed and pitched over the cliff into the sea by United States forces when they took over Greencastle airfield during World War II and cleared its perimetal area. To the west of Slieve Gullion in County Armagh, beside the road at Ballykeel, there is a fine portal grave or dolmen, as the type is commonly called. The portal grave at Ballylesson near Belfast, known locally as

"The Druid's Altar," stands inside a massive neolithic earthwork, 190 meters in diameter and about 3½ meters in height, called "The Giant's Ring."

The more sophisticated builders of the passage graves were a separate and later migrant group which flourished in the Boyne Valley, once part of Ulster, whence some moved northwards into the present province of Ulster as far as its northern coast. They appear to have come to Ireland from Brittany, or even from Portugal, possibly by way of southwestern Britain and Wales. The passage grave builders, who cremated their dead, decorated the surface of the tombs elaborately with esoteric spirals, concentric circles, and zigzags. Such decoration may be seen on passage graves in County Tyrone, one on the summit of a hill in the Knockmany forest and another at Sess Kilgreen. Archeologists have particularly noted the Iberian affinities of the decoration of the grave in the south of County Armagh, on the summit of massive Slieve Gullion, called "Ireland's most mysterious mountain" by the nineteenth-century scholar Standish O'Grady.

In the ancient sagas, the home of Culann, the smith, the most famous sword-maker in Ireland, was on Slieve Gullion. The Ulster Cycle recounts the heroic adventures of Ulster's Cú Chulainn and Queen Maeve of Connacht's cattle raid into Ulster to capture the magnificent brown bull, Donn Cúalnge. Cú Chulainn, the son of a chieftain and of the King of Ulster's sister, was named Setanta as a child. When he overthrew one hundred and fifty opponents at wrestling he attracted the attention of his uncle the King who invited the lad to a feast at the house of Culann. Setanta arrived after the other guests and found the gates locked and the entrance guarded by a dog so savage that it took three men with three chains to hold him. The fierce animal leapt to attack Setanta but the boy dropped his javelin, his hurley stick and ball, seized the dog by the throat and dashed its brains out against a pillar. Culann was, of course, glad that Setanta had not been killed by the dog, but he feared that he would be defenseless without the hound, so Setanta proposed to guard Culann's place himself until he could rear a puppy from the same pack to take the guard dog's place. Consequently, he was renamed Cú Chulainn, meaning "the hound of Culann." As Cú Chulainn, he won his place among the warriors by breaking hunting spears, war spears, and swords, and by proving his expertise as a charioteer. Although small in stature he became a mighty hero, performing wonderful feats of arms. Once, on the Ulster marches, after Maeve had taken the brown bull from the glens of Slieve Gullion,

Cú Chulainn killed almost two hundred enemy chiefs and princes and as many lesser warriors in a single day's battle.

Many nineteenth-century scholars firmly believed in the historicity of Cú Chulainn, his wife Emer, the arrogant Queen Maeve, and other characters in the Ulster Cycle. Now, it is generally accepted that the Irish sagas preserve only the spirit of the embattled relations that existed between the men of Ulster and the men of Connacht. Although the sagas are fictional, the descriptions of society in Ireland in the early Iron Age are of historical interest.

These heroic tales survived because they were eventually transcribed by the early Christian monks. Before that time they had been recited by generations of professional storytellers. The longest and most important heroic tale of the Ulster Cycle, *Táin Bó Cúalnge* (*The Cattle Raid of Cooley*), mentions numerous identifiable places in Ulster, such as the Fews Mountains of County Armagh, the Mourne Mountains of County Down, the Bann and Callan rivers, Dunseverick in northern County Antrim, Assaroe in County Donegal, Farney in County Monaghan, Dun Da Bend (now called Mount Sandel) in County Derry, and the pagan capital of Ulster—Emain Macha, now known as Navan Fort, situated two miles west of Armagh. The pagan civilization that the sagas portray is that of the Celts, who had certainly arrived in Ireland by 500 B.C. and may have begun to arrive several centuries earlier, during the early Bronze Age.

The dawn of the Metal Age about 2000 B.C. brought new immigrants to Ireland, metal prospectors who spread across Europe in their search for new deposits. Among those who came were the Beaker Folk. Evidence of their presence in Ireland was first found on a site in County Derry, Wellglass Cairn. With the new metalworkers in the Bronze Age came new burial customs: individual interments in single graves, usually cairns constructed on the tops of hills. The proliferation of these graves changed the landscape. Throughout the Bronze Age stone circles were erected too, the greatest concentration of these in Ireland being in the uplands of mid-Ulster, where dozens have been found. The most elaborate circles were discovered under peat at Beaghmore near Dunnamore in County Tyrone. The exact purpose of these circles is still obscure, but it is now thought that the builders had some knowledge of astronomy and that the circles may have been calendrical. Sometimes cairns containing cremation burials have been found within or near the circles. At Ballynoe in County Down, an outer circle 35½ meters in diameter with fifty upright stones encloses a smaller, inner circle. The

small circle on the eastern side of Tievebulliagh in Glenaan, County Antrim, is known as Ossian's Grave because of a popular tradition that the megalithic tomb on the site is the burial place of the Celtic poet. A fine Ulster stone circle, of which sixty stones survive, is situated on a hilltop that commands an extensive view at Beltany in County Donegal.

It is not for these stone monuments, however, that Bronze Age and early Iron Age workers are famous, but for their exquisite metal artifacts: decorated flat axes, a speciality of northeastern Ulster, spearheads, daggers, scabbards, horse bits, harness decorations, and gold ornaments such as the torque, a twisted neckband, armband or girdle, flat crescent-shaped collars known as *lunulae,* earrings and discs. In 1896, two men plowing a field found a wonderful cache of precious gold objects at Broighter, near Lough Foyle in County Derry. A hammered gold *lunula* called the Broighter Collar, a unique miniature golden boat complete with mast, oars, and seats (possibly a votive object), two golden torques marvellously decorated with swirls and made with complicated clasps, and two chains of plaited gold wire, all part of the find, are kept in the National Museum, Dublin. At Downpatrick, County Down, sixteen gold bracelets of the late Bronze Age were discovered; and on a crannog in the lake at Lisnacrogher, County Antrim, three bronze sword scabbards were found. These are splendidly decorated in the style known as La Tène, brought by Celtic immigrants in the last centuries B.C. A laborer digging potatoes at Mill Loughan on the east bank of the River Bann in County Derry, in 1855, found a gold penannular brooch, the Dalriada Brooch, now in the National Museum, Dublin. How many such treasures are still buried beneath the soil of Ulster?

Little is known of the beliefs and practices of the Celts in Ireland in the centuries prior to the introduction of Christianity. Some of their carved stones that have been found, apparently pagan cult objects, are as mysterious as the early circles and standing stones. On Boa Island in Lough Erne, County Fermanagh, are the most impressive of these idols; one, a large, neckless figure, has two weird triangular-faced heads, back to back. At Corleck, in the neighboring county of Cavan, a simple three-faced stone head was found.

About A.D. 300, a script was developed known as Ogham, after Ogmios, the Celts' god of writing. This script was formed by placing four sets of from one to five strokes in differing positions in relation to a central line. One set crossed the central line horizontally, the second was placed horizontally to one side of the central line, the third to the other side, and the fourth crossed the line diagonally, thus making twenty letters. Inscriptions carved on stones were meant to be read from the bottom upwards, and if necessary continued on from the top to the bottom on the other side. One example of a stone in Ulster inscribed in Ogham script may be seen at Aghascrebagh in the Owen Killew Valley of the Sperrin Mountains.

The inscrutable statues on White Island in Lough Erne were once thought to be pagan deities, but they are Christian objects; one represents a bishop or an abbess. Although their appearance is pagan, artistically they belong to the transitional period of early Christianity in Ulster. These statues were found built into the walls of a Romanesque church and have now been placed in a row.

The Celtic metal artifacts continued to be manufactured in Ireland after the arrival of Christianity. A bronze strainer perforated with spirals in the La Tène tradition, found on a crannog at Moylarg, County Antrim, dates from the seventh or eighth century. Spirals, scrolls, and trumpet patterns remained popular decorative motifs but, with the conversion of the population to Christianity, craftsmen made reliquaries and copied and illustrated sacred texts.

Patrick, the Christian missionary generally credited with the conversion of the Irish in the fifth century A.D., was mainly active in the northern part of the island. Already by the seventh century, Armagh, claimed to have been his seat, had established an ecclesiastical primacy which has endured to the present day: Armagh is the seat of both the Roman Catholic and the Church of Ireland (Protestant Episcopalian) Primates of all Ireland, both bearing the title of Archbishop of Armagh. Conflicting early sources claim that Patrick was buried at Armagh, and at Downpatrick, the traditional site of his first church. A granite block erected in 1900 in the cemetery of Downpatrick Cathedral supposedly marks the grave of the saint. Patrick, the son of a Christian family living on or near the west coast of Britain, was abducted by pirates and spent six years in pagan Ireland as a slave before he contrived to escape. There is a tradition that he spent his years of slavery herding swine for a pagan chieftain on steep-sided Slemish Mountain, east of Ballymena in County Antrim, but this is discounted by modern scholars.

There are many stories of Patrick's life and labors. Those that recount incidents when his mission was not well received almost certainly reflect historical truth, since not all the chiefs and their followers would have accepted the new beliefs without a tussle. One such story relates the conversion of Donard, a chieftain of Rath Murbolg, now Maghera, in County Down. Donard, who obstinately resisted Patrick's efforts, was only convinced when the saint restored to life a bull which had not only been slaughtered, but also disjointed and salted. Subsequently Donard himself became a fervent believer and proselytizer; he established a monastery at Maghera and is remembered as Saint Donard. His name survives in the mountain, Slieve Donard, on whose summit, for centuries a place of pilgrimage, the saint elected, according to local lore, to reside in a cave until the Day of Judgment. In fact, on the summit of Slieve Donard there is a prehistoric burial cairn, the most ancient mark of man in the Mourne Mountains. This corbeled passage grave appears to have been Saint Donard's cell. A smaller but better preserved cairn situated about 740 meters from the summit is believed to have been his oratory. According to an Early Christian Irish martyrology, Saint Donard died on March 24, 506.

Not surprisingly, the earliest datable Christian monument in Ireland is to be found in Ulster. A carved standing stone on the grounds of a farm at Kilnasaggart, County Armagh, in the vicinity of Slieve Gullion, is incised with crosses and has an inscription recording that it was erected by one Ternoc; this Ternoc, a brother of the Archbishop of Armagh, died in A.D. 714.

The Roman legions that invaded Britain never reached Ireland, so Ireland's Iron Age lasted well into the Christian period. In Ulster, by the time of Patrick's missionary activity, lived the descendants of the Beaker Folk and of the more recently arrived Celtic immigrants together with the ancient pre-Celtic stock, descendants of the first mesolithic fishers and fowlers, of the neolithic farmers, and of the passage grave builders. The very sophistication of the Celtic order has tended to obscure the presence of the older pre-Celtic stock but, as Professor E. Estyn Evans has pointed out, the older stock has left a deeper genetic mark on the Irish population than the Celts, especially in Ulster and parts of the West where a relatively high proportion of the inhabitants are of Blood Group O, indicating pre-Celtic ancestry. In the remoter parts of Ulster both the blood and the habits of the ancient stock persist.

The sagas stress the difference between the "men of Ulster" and the other inhabitants of the island. Archeological findings support this. For example, in the North the people cooked in flat-bottomed pots known as souterrain ware, not found elsewhere in Ireland. The objects relating to the Celtic La Tène culture in the North mostly have British affinities, while many of those found in other parts of the island have more Continental affinities; this may indicate that the Celts in Ulster arrived by a different route and possibly later than those in the South.

Before Armagh became a religious city it may have been a secular site, possibly the capital of Ulster, although the ceremonial center of the kings may have been at Navan Fort, anciently Emain Macha, which appears to have flourished when Armagh, named for the same pagan goddess Macha, was founded only two miles away. The boundaries of the Kingdom of Ulster shrank to include only Antrim, Down, and some of the north of County Louth, now part of Leinster. To the west of this region, the Uí Néill, claiming descent from Niall of the Nine Hostages, eventually established their sway as far as the lordships of the Maguires of Fermanagh and the O'Donnells of Tirconnell. The demise of Emain Macha appears to have coincided with the end of the old Kingdom of Ulster as a dominant power.

Patrick's choice of Armagh would certainly appear to have been dictated by its existing importance. In his missionary endeavors he did not attempt to disturb the contemporary societal patterns, limiting himself to preaching the divinity of Jesus Christ.

The Grianán of Aileach, an imposing stone fort, 71 meters in diameter, was the royal seat of the northern Uí Néill or O'Neills, who ruled over the territory of Aileach; it served them from about the fifth century until the beginning of the twelfth, when it was ransacked by the King of Munster to avenge their destruction of his own seat at Kincora in County Clare. The great fort, with mural chambers in the thickness of its twelve-meter-thick walls, stands on a hilltop near Burt in County Donegal, commanding breathtaking views over Lough Foyle and Lough Swilly. Three low concentric walls, part of the original fortification, encircle the Grianán; access to the interior was through a long, easily guarded, linteled tunnel. Iron Age forts of this type, in which a stone wall enclosed a hilltop area, usually with an encompassing ditch for added protection, often remained in use for centuries.

From the twelfth century until their defeat in 1607, the coronation place of the O'Neills was a stone ring fort of which only the rath now remains, at Tullaghogue, south of Cookstown, in County Tyrone; the inaugural chair or throne of the chiefs stood near the fort.

Three concentric enclosures known as cashels survive of the pre-Christian settlement at Nendrum on Strangford Lough in County Down, where later Saint Mochaoi erected his monastery, with a church, schoolhouse and dwelling-huts within the innermost cashel, and workshops, including those of a potter and a smith, outside it. The earliest Christian churches in Ireland were small edifices of mud or wood. As late as the twelfth century there is the report of Malachy chopping wood at Bangor in County Down for a *duirtheach*, or wooden chapel, constructed of closely fastened smooth planks.

Churches and church property suffered in the internecine wars between the secular families. The offices of many abbots and abbesses were the preserve of a given family that involved them, their monasteries, their churches and their dependents in raids and reprisals between rival families. Church-burning is usually associated with the fierce Viking raiders, but they did not make their first foray into Ireland until A.D. 795. The Annals of Ulster record the burnings of a number of churches within the present limits of the province well before that date, evidently the work of insiders. A church was burned at Bangor in 615 and one at Connor, County Antrim, in the following year. Later in that century churches were burned at Derry, at Bangor, at Coleraine in County Derry, Kilmore, County Cavan, and Inniskeen, County Monaghan. In 809, after an abbot was murdered beside the shrine of Patrick, the O'Neills plundered the Kingdom of Ulster to avenge the desecration.

Ulster's natural land defenses obliged outsiders to take one of only three routes: over the Erne near Ballyshannon or between the upper and lower lakes at Enniskillen on the southwest, and in the southeast through the Moyry Pass, a gorge in the hills between Dundalk and Newry, called the Gateway to Ulster. Northeast Ulster, covered by vast tracts of dense woodland, was virtually impassable. The Vikings, who were skillful navigators, at first only made temporary settlements at a few places such as Narrow Water on the coast of Down, and on the coast of Antrim and Donegal, plundering Rathlin Island, which was accessible, and vulnerable places on the mainland like Bangor. In 825 they sailed into Strangford Lough, reached Downpatrick, and sacked it. In the same year they sailed into Lough Foyle and sacked the monastery founded by Saint Finnian at Moville, now County Donegal. Seven years later, from Carlingford Lough, which was named by the Viking invaders for its resemblance to one of their native fjords, they thrust inland to Armagh, probably following the Bann for some miles before going overland to sack one of the two greatest monasteries in Ireland. The Vikings plundered Armagh again in 868, but the monks saved such treasures as the *Book of Armagh,* a wonderful, illustrated work executed there in and around the year 807. Abbot Torbach, who dictated the text, died at Armagh in 808. The penmanship of the scribe Ferdomnach is exquisite. He drew decorative initials and the vulgate symbols of the four Evangelists. The *Gospels of Mac Durnan,* the property of an abbot of Armagh who held office from 888 to 927 and for whom the work is named, were also written and illustrated at Armagh.

Viking influence can be discerned in a number of Irish artifacts. The artisan of the fine bronze and gold reliquary made to contain Saint Patrick's bell employed decorative elements of the Scandinavian Urnes style.

After the Viking incursions, Brian Ború (Boroimhe), King of Munster, emerged as the most powerful of the regional monarchs in Ireland. In 1001 he took hostages from the reigning High King, Maelseachnaill O'Neill, who had not managed to establish himself. Brian thus wrested the High Kingship from the northern O'Neills and was recognized as High King of Ireland, to whom the other monarchs paid homage. As High King, Brian never disputed Armagh's claim to ecclesiastical supremacy. Indeed, when he visited Armagh in 1005, he confirmed its privileged position and as *Imperator Scotorum* (Emperor of the Irish) had it recorded in the *Book of Armagh.*

Brian died of wounds in the battle at which his armies vanquished the remnants of Viking power in Ireland in 1014, and the struggle for the High Kingship was resumed among the contending families, the O'Briens in the South, the O'Conors in the West, and the O'Neills in the North, but the ecclesiastical overlordship of Armagh was not challenged. Three twelfth-century synods initiated church reforms; at the second of these, the Synod of Rath Bresail in 1110, Cellach, the reigning Bishop of Armagh, established the primacy of the Comarb of Patrick at Armagh. At the Synod of Kells in 1152, a diocesan organization was established with four ecclesiastical provinces, one of which, Armagh, retained the primacy.

Saint Malachy of Armagh, born about 1095, was a leading figure in the reforms. His mentor, Imhar O'Hagan, who died in Rome in 1134, built the Abbey Church of Saint Peter and Saint Paul at Armagh, and in his time too the great stone church at Armagh was reroofed. On returning to Ulster from France and Rome in 1140, Malachy wished to emulate the style of the magnificent churches he had seen on his travels. The saint's friend and biographer, Saint Bernard of Clairvaux, related the building of a stone oratory by Malachy at Bangor in County Down. "When he

began to lay the foundations," the biographer reported, "the natives wondered because in that land no such buildings were yet to be found." A local man reprimanded Malachy for the innovation and Saint Bernard recorded that this onlooker, clearly conservative, asked: "...why have you thought good to introduce this novelty into our regions? ...What is this frivolity?" Stone churches with decorative elements were built in Ulster, nevertheless. Examples survive, dating at least from the twelfth century, in County Derry, at Dungiven and at Banagher; and at Maghera, in the same county, there is a stone church door with decorative carving on the jambs, facings and architrave, and a crucifixion scene sculpted in relief on the massive lintel, apparently also twelfth-century. However, the Hiberno-Romanesque architecture which flourished farther south is rare in Ulster, and survives only in the south of the present province: a single doorway of the ruined stone church on White Island, County Fermanagh, built over an earlier wooden church in the twelfth century; and one much grander door believed to have been part of the original Premonstratensian abbey on Trinity Island in Lough Oughter, County Cavan, now in Ulster but formerly in Connacht. (Built into the seventeenth-century Church of Ireland Cathedral at Kilmore, County Cavan, it is incorporated in the present cathedral as the vestry door.)

The first Norman knights who arrived in Ireland from Britain with their soldiers in 1169 landed in south Leinster, but only eight years later, John de Courcy, with a small army, marched north into Ulster. He took Downpatrick by surprise, rapidly defeated the King of Ulster and established himself as the virtual ruler of the territory he conquered east of the Bann—the southeastern part of the present province. Although he plundered Armagh in 1189 and made successful forays into what is now County Donegal, de Courcy was not able to extend his territory beyond the Bann. To consolidate his hold, he threw up motte-and-bailey fortifications at such strategic points as the Mount at Hilltown, a steep artificial mound on which stood a wooden tower enclosed by a palisade and a ditch. This particular fortification guarded a ford over the Upper Bann and controlled the foothill route from east to west across the Mournes as well as ways through the mountains. Another of de Courcy's earthworks that changed the landscape was the mound at Newry. Another, a small motte near the sea at Greencastle, County Down, was used in conjunction with a fort across the water at Carlingford, to command the all-important entry to Carlingford Lough. At Dundrum, de Courcy used a prehistoric hilltop rath for a motte, a natural mound on top of a hill 185 meters high, around which he erected a strong polygonal curtain wall. This fort overlooked the inner bay, the plains of Lecale and the pass between the Mountains of Mourne and the foothills of Slieve Croob. Farther north, on a rocky promontory that juts out into Belfast Lough at Carrickfergus, de Courcy began the construction of a more substantial stone castle in the 1180s.

With great ruthlessness de Courcy destroyed religious foundations as he passed. With the shrewdness of the colonizer and with one eye on heaven, he replaced them with new ones, and imported ecclesiastics on whose loyalty he could count. He built a new cathedral friary at Downpatrick and established Benedictines from Chester there in 1183. For Black Abbey, near Innishargy, also in County Down, he brought over Benedictines from Somerset in the west of England, and from Normandy. In the old Celtic monastery at Nendrum he placed Benedictines from Cumberland in northern England. Together with his wife Affrica, a daughter of the King of the Isle of Man, de Courcy also endowed two Cistercian foundations on his lands in Ulster, one of which, at Inch, near Downpatrick, replaced the monastery of Erinagle which he had destroyed. Cistercians were brought from Lancashire for this abbey, the ruins of which survive. There are also extensive remains of the other de Courcy Cistercian foundation in County Down, Grey Abbey, for which monks were brought from Cumberland in 1193.

John de Courcy excited the suspicion and fear of his lawful sovereign, King John, who confiscated de Courcy's territory and granted it as the Earldom of Ulster to Hugh de Lacy. De Lacy consolidated the Anglo-Norman hold of the territory by building stone castles on some of the fortress sites. But no sooner was his great unbuttressed four-story keep at Carrickfergus nearing completion than the King decided to curb the power of this mighty subject too. He besieged the castle in 1210, took it, and kept it for the Crown. The same year King John visited Dundrum Castle and arranged for building there to continue. The castles at Greencastle and Carlingford, of which there are substantial remains, were fitted up for the Crown as fortresses in the thirteenth century.

The Anglo-Normans redivided the land and introduced administrative changes in their territory in southeast Ulster. The petty kingdoms held by the Irish clans for whom they were named were replaced by land divisions based on the counties of England and given the name of an urban settlement. The castles became the centers of manors where a flourishing agriculture developed. In the process of colonization, knights and lesser settlers, as well as foreign clerics, came to the Earldom of Ulster. In some areas feudal relationships superseded the kinship ties of the Celtic system. However, settlers also became hibernicized to a degree. The Savage family, who arrived in the Ards region of County Down as early as 1177, and whose descendants are still to be found in the area, eventually became as Irish as the Irish. However, where the Anglo-Normans failed to penetrate west of the Bann, in Tirowen, ruled by the O'Neills, and Tirconnell, ruled by the O'Donnells, and in the inaccessible glens of Antrim, the ancient way of life remained unaffected by the alien culture of the invaders.

In 1314 Robert Bruce, King of Scotland, fresh from his triumph over the English at Bannockburn, embarked on a project to create a united Gaelic kingdom of Scotland and Ireland, with his brother Edward Bruce as the King of Ireland. He was supported by a number of the Ulster chiefs who realized the advantage of uniting against their common enemy, the Crown of England. When Edward Bruce landed in Ulster in 1315 with six thousand troops from Scotland he was joined by five Ulster chieftains: O'Neill of Tirowen, O'Kane, Lord of Keenaght, O'Hanlon, whose territory was in the present County Armagh, O'Hagan of Tullaghogue in County Tyrone, and Mac Cartan of Kinelearty in County Down. In their first march south they sacked Dundalk and pushed as far as Ardee. After retreating to the north they marched south again, this time reaching Kildare. Edward Bruce was crowned King of Ireland but he made a tactical error by not marching on Dublin; instead he turned back to Ulster and made Carrickfergus Castle his headquarters. There he was joined by his brother Robert with a large army; together they marched south, destroying the monastery at Downpatrick and sacking Greencastle. They thrust deep into the southwest of Ireland, but although they were at Castleknock on the outskirts of Dublin, again it was decided not to attack the city and instead they turned back to Carrickfergus. When Edward Bruce marched south once again the Crown had had time to consolidate its forces; moreover, the Pope, who championed the English King, had excommunicated Bruce and his allies, thereby undermining the support of the Irish chieftains. An army with the Primate Archbishop of Armagh at its head defeated Edward Bruce's forces at Dundalk and he was slain in battle. Robert Bruce's dream of a Gaelic kingdom in Ireland was ended, but not the desire of the Ulster chieftains to rid themselves of the English presence.

Fourteenth-century Ulster was divided territorially into five main states. To the west, Tirconnell, which comprised most of the present county of Donegal, was under the O'Donnells and their subchiefs, of whom the most prominent were the O'Boyles and the O'Dohertys. The Ulster chieftains engaged mercenaries, called gallowglasses, many of whom came over from Scotland and established themselves in Ulster, the ancient place of origin of many of their ancestors. One of these gallowglass families, the fiery Mac Sweeneys, who had arrived in the thirteenth century, became powerful in the north and west of Tirconnell where the O'Donnells granted them lands in payment for their services. Other prominent families of Tirconnell were the O'Friels, descendants of a brother of Saint Columcille, who enjoyed the hereditary right to inaugurate the reigning O'Donnell as ruler of Tirconnell on the Rock of Doon; the O'Shiels, a family of hereditary physicians; the Mac Wards, hereditary bards; and the MacLoughlins. There were also refugee families like the Mac Dunlevys and Mac Gillespies, who had been dispossessed of their lands in eastern Ulster by the newcomers and reestablished themselves in Tirconnell under the O'Donnells. The Mac Roartys or O'Roartys, comarbs (hereditary ecclesiastical successors) of Saint Columcille on Tory Island, the Mac Graths of Termon Mac Grath, and the Mac Gonigles were distinguished ecclesiastical families. Other families owed their position to their role as erenaghs (hereditary custodians of church lands or relics). Among these were the O'Mulhollands of Loughinsholin, County Derry, keepers of Saint Patrick's bell, the O'Strahans, O'Harkans, and O'Derrys.

Tirowen, under the O'Neills, was larger than the present county of Tyrone as it included also a part of what is now County Derry. Formerly all of the present county of Derry was part of Tirowen, but the Crown-controlled Earldom of Ulster had usurped the region east of Lough Foyle and up to the northern coast. Next to the O'Neills the most powerful families were the O'Cahans or O'Kanes, Lords of Keenaght, in what is now County Derry, and the O'Hagans of Tullaghogue, who enjoyed the hereditary privilege of inaugurating the reigning O'Neill. Other prominent Tirowen families, most of whose names survive in the region, were the O'Quinns, O'Donnellys, O'Hamills, Mac Gurks, Mac Murphys, O'Hegartys, O'Devlins, O'Lunneys of Munterlooney, Mac Gilmartins, Mac Gettigans, Mac Closkys, Mac Colgans, O'Carolans of Clondermot, O'Mulvennas, Mac Gilligans, and O'Lavertys. The Mac Namees were a family of hereditary poets and ollavs. The O'Dimonds, Mac Crillys, or O'Crillys and O'Mellans were important erenagh families.

Fermanagh was the lordship of the Maguires. The O'Husseys were their hereditary bards, the O'Keenans their historians, the O'Cassidys their physicians and ollavs, and the O'Breslins their legal experts in the Brehon laws which governed Gaelic society. The O'Slevins and O'Corcorans were ecclesiastical families, and the Mac Carberys of Galloon and the O'Drumms of Kinawley the leading erenaghs. Other Fermanagh families of note were the once powerful Mac Mulrooneys, who had been subjugated by the Maguires, the Mac Manus sept, who like the Mac Auleys and Mac Corrys were a branch of the Maguires, the Mac Kiernans, Mac Gilroys, O'Bannons, Mac Entegarts, and O'Muldoons.

Oriel or Uriel covered most of the present counties of Armagh and Monaghan and parts of what are now the counties of Down and Louth, as well as a small area of the eastern part of County Fermanagh. Here the most prominent families were the Mac Mahons, the O'Hanlons, the O'Keelaghans, the McCanns of Clanbrassil, the O'Boylans of Dartry, and the Mac Kennas of Truagh. In Oriel the Mac Parlans were famous as poets and scribes, the O'Loughrans as an ecclesiastical family, and the Mac Cosgraves of Clones as erenaghs. Among the septs established in Oriel were the Mac Ardles, who were a branch of the Mac Mahons, the O'Garveys, a branch of the O'Hanlons, the O'Hanrattys, O'Callans, O'Larkins, O'Donegans, O'Mulcreevys, O'Heaneys, Mac Alindens, Mac Entees or Mac Gintys, O'Hoeys, Mac Nallys, Mac Veaghs, Mac Eneanys, Mac Mackins, O'Herans, O'Rogans, and the O'Duffys. O'Duffy or Duffy is the commonest name in County Monaghan today.

In the Earldom of Ulster, the Gaelic system had broken down under English control although it had not disappeared. Some of the original families had moved west but a few, like the Mac Guinness family of Iveagh, remained. Some Norman families, like the Savages of the Ards, and to a greater extent the MacQuillans, Lords of the Route in northern Antrim, descended from the Norman family of Mandeville, had become hibernicized. In the remote glens of Antrim, where the Gaelic way of life endured, the Mac Donnells, a gallowglass family, held sway. Other gallowglass families settled in the Glens were the Bissells who became Mac Keowns, the Mac Neills who arrived early in the fourteenth century, and the Mac Alisters, along with migrant families from Connacht, the Mac Clearys and O'Haras. A branch of the O'Neills, the

Clann Aodh Bhuidhe, also settled in Antrim at that time.

Economic troubles and disease plagued Ireland in the century after the Bruce debacle. Meanwhile, the anger of the Ulster chieftains simmered, and skirmishes with the authorities and forays into the Earldom were not infrequent. It was the events of the sixteenth century, however, that incited them to full-scale rebellion.

The policy of the Tudor monarchs to extend the royal writ throughout Ireland, and the means by which they attempted to anglicize the Irish, alarmed the Gaelic lords. At first, they were less perturbed by England's break with Rome. The Act of Parliament that proclaimed Henry VIII "only supreme head on earth of the whole Church of Ireland," passed almost unnoticed. It was the accession of Elizabeth I, rejected by the Pope as a bastard and a heretic, that brought matters to a head.

The Pope, who recognized King Philip of Spain, the widower of Elizabeth's sister, Mary I, as the lawful King of England and Ireland, issued a Bull in 1570 absolving the Irish of allegiance to Elizabeth. This, of course, incited the Ulster chieftains to rebellion.

In 1569 the Crown abolished the sovereignty of the O'Neills and backed an attempt at colonization in the north of Ireland. The attempt, led by Sir Thomas Smith and his son, to plant Protestant English farmers in the Ards of County Down, was a failure, and so too was the bloody attempt by the Earl of Essex in County Antrim. Essex murdered two hundred O'Neill followers at Belfast and had Sir Brian MacPhelim O'Neill and his wife hanged and quartered. Sir Francis Drake, more often remembered as a gallant English naval hero, took part in Essex's attack on Rathlin Island off the north coast of Antrim, where the MacDonnells had sent their womenfolk and children for safety. The English force trapped them on the island and massacred them.

The brutalities, the attempted settlements, the policy of surrender and regrant, whereby the chieftains were urged to surrender the clan lands to the Crown and have them regranted under English law, were all major irritants to the Gaelic chieftains and their people. The surrender and regrant policy meant that the estates would henceforth pass by primogeniture. This was totally contrary to the Gaelic system whereby the lands belonged jointly to all members of the clan as parceners; they selected the most able member of the leading family to succeed as chief.

The English Queen was regarded by the Gaelic Irish as the enemy of their whole way of life; the fact that she was also the enemy of their Faith only made things worse. In their desire to overthrow this archenemy, chieftains like the O'Neill looked to the enemies of their enemy for allies; to the Pope, the Spanish, and the French.

The Spaniards made an attempt to invade England and overthrow Elizabeth in 1588, but their Armada was defeated and scattered. The Spanish fleet, unable to turn back, made for home by sailing north around Scotland and Ireland into the Atlantic. If the beleaguered Spanish admirals could have contacted their King he might have decided to order them to land in Ulster and join O'Neill, although it appears that he was never convinced by the pleas of the Ulster chieftains to undermine Elizabeth's power by helping them to drive the English out of Ireland. As it was, supplies were dangerously low, many of their men were sick, and the admirals must have been torn between the choice of stopping for help in Ulster and pushing as fast as possible for home. In an attempt to make for Spain, at least twenty-four Spanish ships were wrecked around the treacherous Irish coast and two more went down far out to sea, with a total loss of about five thousand men. One proud galleon, the *Girona,* was wrecked on the north Antrim coast at a spot remembered as Spanish Point. In 1967 and 1968, a diving team reached this wreck and brought up almost ten thousand objects, including beautiful jewelry, cameos and gold chains, which are now on display in the Ulster Museum at Belfast.

O'Neill continued his negotiations with King Philip of Spain who, despite the defeat of his Invincible Armada, was still anxious to overthrow Elizabeth. Meanwhile, in Ulster, as soon as the Crown had negotiated surrender and regrant arrangements with the Mac Mahons and the Mac Kennas in Monaghan, the O'Donnell of Tirconnell and the Maguire of Fermanagh swept down and raided the estates, and in 1594 they routed an English force sent to suppress them. In 1595 they were joined by the O'Neill, who had been fitting up an efficient army, which defeated the English at Clontibret, County Monaghan. In 1597 O'Neill and his allies inflicted a further defeat on their enemy at the Battle of the Yellow Ford on the Callan River, in County Armagh.

The rebellion was now in full swing and O'Neill counted among his allies some of the Irish chiefs who had been hesitant to join the rebels. However, the Spaniards were slow to move. Had they come in time, before the English had reassembled an efficient army, the course of Irish history might have been different. Understandably, the Spaniards had bad memories of Ireland, for not only had thousands of their men been drowned in its seas, but of those who struggled to shore, many were apprehended and killed by the English, or assaulted and robbed of what they had salvaged, and even murdered by the wilder Irish.

In 1600, with the blessing of the Pope, who granted a plenary pardon and remission of all sins to all who joined him, O'Neill marched at the head of a refitted army into Westmeath. But some of his allies fell away and the Crown had had time to assemble and equip a force of twenty thousand men. At the Moyry Pass, the English succeeded in forcing O'Neill's army to retreat into Ulster. O'Neill was probably not discouraged because the Spaniards had agreed to send a sizable force. However, the Spanish fleet encountered bad weather and their admiral brought his ships into port on the south coast. This meant that O'Neill, O'Donnell, and their followers had to march the length of Ireland to join their allies. Outside their familiar territory they were at a disadvantage, and the English defeated them. O'Donnell fled at once to Spain. O'Neill returned to Ulster to make a last stand but was forced to submission in 1603 and, to avoid humiliation, or the fate of the O'Cahan, who died in the Tower of London, went into exile with one hundred Ulster leaders. Their departure, remembered as the Flight of the Earls, was lamented by the bards.

The Maguire's bard, Eochaidh O'Hussey, began his mournful ode with these words (in translation):

Where is my Chief, my master, this bleak night, mavrone!
O, Cold, cold, miserably cold is this bleak night for Hugh,
Its showery, arrowy, speary sleet pierceth one through and
    through—
Pierceth one to the very bone!

The ode ends with its touching envoi:

Hugh marched forth to the fight—I grieved to see him so
    depart;
And lo! tonight he wanders frozen, rain-drenched, sad,
    betrayed—
But the memory of the limewhite mansions his right hand
Hath laid in ashes, warms the hero's heart.

Robin Flower, a twentieth-century English scholar of Irish, has translated the lament of Aindrais Mac Marcuis entitled *This Night Sees Ireland Desolate*, as follows:

This night sees Eire desolate,
Her chiefs are cast out of their state;
Her men, her maidens weep to see
Her desolate that should peopled be.

How desolate is Connla's Plain,
Though aliens swarm in her domain;
Her rich bright soil had joy in these
That now are scattered overseas.

Man after man, day after day
Her noblest princes pass away
And leave to all the rabble rest
A land dispeopled of her best.

O'Donnell goes. In that stern strait
Sore-stricken Ulster mourns her fate,
And all the northern shore makes moan
To hear that Aodh of Annagh's gone.

Men smile at childhood's play no more,
Music and song, their day is o'er;
At wine, at Mass the kingdom's heirs
Are seen no more; changed hearts are theirs.

They feast no more, they gamble not,
All goodly pastime is forgot,
They barter not, they race no steeds,
They take no joy in stirring deeds.

No praise in builded song expressed
They hear, no tales before they rest;
None care for books and none take glee
To hear the long-traced pedigree.

The packs are silent, there's no sound
Of the old strain on Bregian ground.
A foreign flood holds all the shore,
And the great wolf-dog barks no more.

Woe to the Gael in this sore plight!
Henceforth they shall not know delight.
No tidings now their woe relieves,
Too close the gnawing sorrow cleaves.

These the examples of their woe;
Israel in Egypt long ago,
Troy that the Greek hosts set on flame,
And Babylon that to ruin came.

Sundered from hope, what friendly hand
Can save the sea-surrounded land?

The clan of Conn no Moses see
To lead them from captivity.

Her chiefs are gone. There's none to bear
Her cross or lift her from despair;
The grieving lords take ship. With these
Our very souls pass overseas.

The Tirconnell bard, Fearghal Oge Mac Ward, composed a long dirge, *The Flight of the Earls*, which poignantly expresses the feelings of the people. It has been beautifully translated by the late Earl of Longford, as the following extract shows:

All Ireland's now one vessel's company,
And riding west by cliffs of Beare to sea.
Upon the snowy foam of the ebbing tide
Away in one frail bark goes all our pride.
Now stolen is the soul from Eire's breast,
And all her coasts and islands mourn oppressed.
The great twin eagles of the flock of Conn
In perilous flight are in one vessel gone.
For they whose pinions shaded Ulster's plain
In their high bark have gone nor come again;
Two last and yet most royal birds of all
Fly westward to the sea beyond recall...
Rory our darling, and our most gracious Hugh!
And tho' we named no names beyond the two,
Yet in this sailing have we lost a host
Of men that fainting Ireland needed most...

Now let the hearts of all rejoice again,
For our great Earls have safely come to Spain;
And yet their going o'er the sea must fill
With bitter wailing Eire's every hill.
Comparing their good fortune, being away,
With their sad impotence if they should stay,
Let Uisneach's land lament and yet rejoice,
And gloom and glory mingle now their voice.
And yet to know that they are gone from me,
And sail with good success beyond the sea,
Has left me lying in affliction sore.
Alas, for them, for me, for evermore!

The hearts of those that were left turned toward Spain; the territories of the Ulster clans were confiscated by the Crown and an entire new order was instituted which radically changed both the society and much of the landscape of the province forever, for until then even the Earldom of Ulster had only been superficially anglicized and few radical changes had been made.

Nearly four million acres of confiscated estates fell to the Crown, of which about one and a half million were very poor or totally barren land. This bad, infertile land was allotted to the native Irish population, who were consequently compelled to an underprivileged existence. Thus were sown the seeds of a deep discontent that is still with us.

Substantial grants of the good land enriched the established Protestant church and grants were made also to other arms and agencies of the Establishment such as the Royal Schools and the military forts. As one part of the vast and intensive plantation program the City of London Livery Companies were invited to back a colony in the county of Coleraine, which was renamed in their honor, by adding London to the Irish name Derry. The London companies such as the Vintners, Drapers, and Mercers laid out neat villages on their estates; cagework houses with exposed beams in the English style were built in orderly rows, as well as an English-style church for the new community. Towns were laid out on a radial pattern with the central diamond which remains such a typical feature of the Ulster town, or, less frequently, on a grid pattern with a central square. The companies' principal town, Londonderry, had four principal streets meeting at the markethouse, and in 1628 a fine church in the style of the London City churches was built. The unique plans of the towns and villages of Ulster are one of its most agreeable legacies from the resettlement of the early seventeenth century; until then there were only two urban developments in the whole province, both towns in the southeast, in the Earldom of Ulster: Newry, County Down, where the first new Protestant church in Ireland was built in 1579, and Carrickfergus, County Antrim. The new towns grew slowly. By the mid-eighteenth century Londonderry had only 8,000 inhabitants and Belfast only 8,500.

The Articles of Plantation issued in 1609 regulated the Plantation of Ulster. Estates of 1,000, 1,500, and 2,000 acres were rented to English and Scots Protestant Landlords (called Undertakers) on the condition that they only allowed English or Scots tenants on their estates. Those who were granted a 2,000-acre holding were obliged to bring over a minimum of forty-eight tenant farmers from England or

Scotland. Land at a higher rental was let to a second category called servitors, mostly government or military men, who in some instances were permitted to have Irish tenants. Smaller estates of about one hundred to three hundred acres could be rented by the native Irish, but they had to pay a much higher rental.

In the first ten years of the Plantation, about forty thousand Scots came to West Ulster. An energetic Scot, James Hamilton, who organized a settlement in the northwest of County Down, alone brought over ten thousand Scots. Consequently many of the commonest Scots names like Boyd, Frazer, Lindsay, Johnston, Morrison, Patterson, and Maxwell are now widespread in Ulster. Among other prominent settler families were the Mac Causlands in Derry and Tyrone, Buchanans and Galbraiths in Tyrone, Aughmutys in Cavan, Achesons, Irwins and Lowthers in Fermanagh, Leslies in Monaghan, Macartneys, Fullertons, Saundersons, Weirs, Conynghams, Alexanders, and Shaws.

The first permanent settler families of the period, like the Uptons who came from England to County Antrim, arrived just before the turn of the century. Another English settler, Sir Arthur Chichester, headed a large private plantation in County Antrim for which he brought tenants and workers from England. Among the other prominent new English landlords in Ulster were the Coles, Archdales and Nixons in County Fermanagh, the Blackers in County Armagh, Anketells and Shirleys in County Monaghan, Clotworthys in County Antrim, and the Annesleys and Hills in County Down. In their wake came many English tenants, so that common English names such as Bradford, Bradshaw, Watson, Taylor, Walker, Jackson, Wilson, Johnson, and Young have been common in Ulster for the last three hundred and fifty years.

For these settlers, loyalty to the Crown and attachment to the tenets of the Reformation were absolute. To them, Rome represented a dual evil, religious and political, the enemy of true Christian belief and practice, and the enemy of the state, ever-ready to intrigue in alliance against it with foreign enemy powers. Indirectly, but obviously, Rome threatened their status quo and their livelihood in the colony. During the struggle for the Crown between the Catholic James II and his Protestant nephew and son-in-law, William of Orange, decisive battles were fought in Ireland; the English and Scots settlers fought heroically for William, knowing that a victory for James could mean the end of their tenure in their new homeland. William III became, and still is, a Protestant hero in Ulster where statues of "King Billy" are raised annually to celebrate his victory. Orange, the name of his royal house, became the symbol of Protestant solidarity. The fact that the Pope, because of shifting continental European alliances, actually favored William against James has been conveniently forgotten by both sides.

To the original inhabitants of Ulster the presence of the settlers was objectionable. They were regarded as land-grabbing intruders, alien heretics who spoke a foreign language and reviled the true faith.

Over the centuries these attitudes hardened. Due to the expansion of the population and the high rents exacted by the landlords, many poor settler descendants were also economically depressed. The Presbyterians, of whom there were many, also suffered civil disadvantages at the hands of the Establishment against which they chafed. In the eighteenth century, Presbyterian protest groups, the Oak Boys and the Steel Boys, also known as the Hearts of Oak and Hearts of Steel, broke out in insurrection because of their grievances over unfair taxes, tithes, and rents. In the rising of 1798, insurgents, carrying firearms, pitchforks, scythes, reaping-hooks and even sharpened harrow pins, wore green cockades. To the alarm of the Establishment, who executed, flogged or transported the men they caught, a number of Presbyterians embraced Irish patriot ideals.

Humane men like the Reverend Steel Dickson, the Presbyterian minister of Portaferry, County Down, decried the distrust and division and declared "Let these bands of wickedness then be broken which bind down our Catholic brethren to contempt, slavery and wretchedness. Let their heavy burdens be undone and their yoke broken...the blessing of God shall unite us as brethren." Mr. Dickson was imprisoned for his efforts and he died a ruined man.

The fragile stability of Ulster ultimately depended on the nerve of the ruling landlord class, who decided to win over the Presbyterians with concessions, so that, despite their common grievances, the underprivileged Presbyterian descendants of settlers and the underprivileged Roman Catholic descendants of the original inhabitants did not forge an alliance, but were kept apart by a barrier of suspicion and intolerance. Even the towns had English, Scots, and Irish quarters, and today in some urban areas of Ulster the two groups continue to live in different neighborhoods, segregated as they have been since the Plantation.

In Ulster, social and religious prejudices, almost inextricably mixed, are still rife. An outsider can be surprised to hear a well-educated, prosperous Presbyterian Ulster matron who has expressed liberal and progressive ideas in many spheres, remark confidentially that the Catholic Irish are superstitious, shiftless, lazy, or dirty, possibly all four. While decrying sectarian violence and religious discrimination, and expressing qualified disapproval of the Orange Lodge, she may wrinkle her nose at mention of a Catholic family with eleven children. Others, with deeper tribal roots, regard the burgeoning Catholic population as a menace. In the rural areas many a Protestant farmer is willing to accept a lower price for his land from a fellow Protestant rather than let it fall into Catholic hands. There are parts of Ulster where a "mixed" marriage still entails flight, but in 1978, to the pleasure of many and the dismay of not a few, David Cook, a Protestant member of the Alliance Party with a Roman Catholic wife, Fionnuala, was installed as the first non-Unionist Lord Mayor of Belfast.

Of course, there are some genuinely unprejudiced people in Northern Ireland who have succeeded in crossing the tribal boundaries. Unfortunately, such instances are rare; in moments of crisis, or at a showdown, there is a widespread retreat behind these tribal lines. In the summer of 1978 the Roman Catholic Primate and Archbishop of Armagh, Dr. Tomás Ó Fiach, publicized the conditions of Republican (Provo) prisoners in Ulster, and gave qualified support to some of their demands. At once all the old suspicions were aroused. The Archbishop revealed his tribal origins by tactlessly referring to the prisoners as "the lads." Protestant Unionists saw the Archbishop's action as the intolerable meddling of the Roman Catholic Church; they condemned the Archbishop as a partisan of the Provos; Presbyterian and Church of Ireland leaders decried Dr. Ó Fiach's statement; there were Orange mutterings about Provos being absolved of murder in the confessional; Provo-supporters, Nationalists, and anti-Brits generally, seized on the statement as an unqualified endorsement of their activities. Very few people cared to examine the actual demands of the prisoners objectively.

So, with both sides remaining behind, or ready to retreat behind, their tribal barriers, the stalemate in Ulster continues. The last verse of Maurice Craig's *Ballad to a Traditional Refrain* sums up this situation:

> O the bricks they will bleed and the rain it will weep,
> And the damp Lagan fog lull the city to sleep;
> It's to hell with the future and live on the past:
> May the Lord in His Mercy be kind to Belfast.

Although most Ulster Protestants no longer voice fears of dark papist plots, or admit openly that they believe the doctrine of transubstantiation to be downright wicked, nevertheless, their mistrust lies not far below the surface, because sectarianism has been purposefully fostered by a church-state-landlord bloc, which had every reason to divide the angry underprivileged and prevent them from discovering their common interests.

The fear, ridiculous as it may seem outside Ulster, is very real. The more liberal Protestant who will attend interchurch meetings is often unwilling to attend one in a Roman Catholic church. The meeting will be held in a Protestant church or neutral secular building. At the other extreme there are fanatics like the Reverend Ian Paisley of the splinter Free Presbyterian Church who, in 1978, attended a Roman Catholic Mass at Westminster together with other members of the British Parliament only to interrupt it "in the name of the Lord Jesus Christ" and solemnly declare the proceedings to be blasphemous. In her book on Northern Ireland, *A Place Apart*, published in 1978, Dervla Murphy relates the equally disquieting although amusing incident of a Protestant schoolboy in Ulster who fled from an interschool state examination in spoken French when he found that the examiner was a nun. He was comforted afterwards by his irate mother, who declared, "Quite right, son. No child of mine will ever be examined by a Taig."

In Ulster newspapers, advertisers for accommodation to let, or situations vacant, sometimes specify that a "Christian" tenant, lodger or employee is sought. Here "Christian" is used as a code word for Protestant.

And what of Roman Catholic bigotry and intransigence? It seems to reside mainly in a refusal to understand the Protestants' concern that as a minority in a united Ireland their personal liberties might be subjected to the influence of a hierarchy bent on imposing Roman Catholic mores; also in an arrogant inability to accept that the Protestant community (which, after all, has been in Ulster longer than the whites have been in the United States), is now Irish. This stems from an Irish Nationalist attitude that ancient Irish ancestry, attachment to the Irish language, and Roman Catholicism, are essential ingredients of true Irishry. The Protestant graffiti in Ulster "NO POPE HERE" (to which one Belfast wag added "LUCKY OLD POPE") are countered with their opponents' graffiti: "BRITS OUT"; although this refers, of course, immediately to the British army, and only obliquely to the pro-British population as a whole. There is also an inclination on the part of some of the Roman Catholic population of Ulster to blame any and all social and economic ills, such as high unemployment, on an administration that has certainly discriminated against them in the past. "No chance of the government improving the harbor here for us and the people on Rathlin Island," says the *Ballycastle* skipper. "We're the wrong colour. The money goes where the Unionist votes come from." In recent years, in an effort to rectify past injustices the authorities have channeled funds into Catholic urban projects, but in rural minority areas there is still a strong feeling of neglect.

There is also a small minority who live in Ulster in voluntary isolation—the British Civil Servants sent over to run the administrative machinery of the Northern Ireland Office. A tightly knit group, they live with their dependents in the agreeable houses assigned to them in suburban Belfast, remaining as aloof from the local society as if they were serving in Borneo or the Solomon Islands.

In the eighteenth century all branches of linen manufacture, for which the most important market was Lurgan, County Armagh, made up an ubiquitous home industry in Ulster, and the bleaching green was a feature of many homesteads, but the linen yarn was mostly exported to England and not made into cloth in the province. Belfast grew as a large and handsome city in the Victorian era due to the extraordinary industrial development of the Lagan Valley with prosperous mills and shipyards. Today the six Ulster counties in Northern Ireland have the highest poverty level in the British Isles and the highest unemployment figure, with one person in nearly two hundred receiving the State family income supplement against one in eight hundred in Britain. In the three Ulster counties in the Irish Republic farm incomes are low. In 1977, Leinster and Munster farm incomes increased over the previous year by 44 percent and in Connacht by 1 percent, while farm incomes in the Ulster counties of Donegal, Monaghan and Cavan actually dropped by 16 percent. The national average income increased in the Republic over all sectors by 30 percent in the same period. Industrial development arrived late in these border counties, but where it has arrived it has changed the economic scene. Pat McGoldrick has described Clones, County Monaghan, for example, as "groaning with poverty" only a few years ago, "a monument to economic incompetence." Now the bacon, textile, meat-packing, and gas container-tank factories provide needed employment and have transformed the scene.

In towns all over Ulster, north and south of the border,

the supermarket has made its appearance. However, many people will be saddened by the disappearance of the butcher, or fletcher, as he is often called in Ulster, the grocer, the draper, and the hardware store. A surprising number of delightful old shopfronts survive in Ireland, where they have a significant place in the landscape. In Belfast, Smyth's sweet shop is a delightful survivor of the bombs and of commercial change, with its wonderful display of homemade old-fashioned confectionery: nutty lumps, lemon drops, flat lumps, coconut ice, toffee apples, freshly made honeycomb, raspberry lumps, and yellow man, an Ulster speciality remembered in the words of John McAuley's popular song:

> Did you treat your Mary Ann
> To dulse and yellow man
> At the Ould Lammas Fair in Ballycastle-O?

But the fishsellers whose cry, "Herrins alive fresh and stinkin'/Come to the cart and see them winkin'," could be heard in the coastal towns and villages of County Down until not long ago, seem to have vanished, ousted by frozen fish fingers.

An attempt has been made at the Folk Museum at Cultra, County Down, opened in 1964, to record and illustrate the vanishing folkways of Ulster, the games and customs that originate in pre-Christian rituals and beliefs, the festivals and fairs. Rural buildings have been reconstructed: a spade mill, a linen scutch mill, a blacksmith's forge, farm dwellings and a weaver's house with a hand loom. At Camphill, between Omagh and Newtownstewart, the Ulster-American Folk Park has been created by the Northern Ireland administration with funds from the Mellon family, whose emigrant ancestor Thomas Mellon left for America in 1818 from a cottage on this site. This Folk Park helps to recall the great Ulster emigration to North America and especially that of the dissatisfied descendants of the seventeenth-century plantation settlers, the so-called Scots-Irish, who went in their thousands in the eighteenth and nineteenth centuries. Among the many descendants of these hardworking emigrants who achieved fame in the United States was John Dunlap, who printed the Declaration of Independence, General Sam Houston, General "Stonewall" Jackson, and the paternal forebears of at least seven presidents of the United States: Andrew Jackson, Andrew Johnson, James Buchanan, Chester Alan Arthur, William McKinley, James Monroe, and Woodrow Wilson, as well as the maternal forebears of others, including James Knox Polk, and Theodore Roosevelt, whose mother's family, the Bullocks, emigrated from the north of County Antrim.

The bulk of Roman Catholic emigration from Ulster was in the nineteenth century in the wake of the Famine. In many parts of the province agrarian conditions were appalling and the people lived at the lowest subsistence level even before the Famine, perhaps nowhere worse than in Gweedore, a largely desolate wasteland of blanket bog in northwest Donegal, where until 1834 there was not a road fit for a wheeled vehicle. The ancient Irish land tenure system called Rundale persisted in this remote place. Each tenant of a townland was entitled to a portion of each kind of land so that instead of one small workable holding, a man would hold thirty or forty scattered plots, too numerous and too small to be fenced or ditched and all at the mercy of the cattle who could trample and devour at will.

In 1837, Patrick McKye, a schoolmaster in this region who had traveled throughout Ulster and been in England, Scotland, Canada, and the United States, reported that the four thousand inhabitants of his Donegal parish, all Roman Catholics, were in a more needy, hungry, and naked condition than any people he had seen anywhere. Incredibly, there were only one cart and one plow in the whole parish and no other vehicle of any sort. In the way of farm implements the four thousand wretches had between them sixteen harrows, twenty shovels, and thirty-two rakes; not one person had a bonnet or boots or such a luxury as a clock, and there were only eight candlesticks, two feather beds, eight chaff beds and ninety-three chairs altogether, in the seven hundred dwellings. Entire families slept huddled together naked, the great majority of them on beds of straw or rushes. Hardly any of the dwellings had a glazed window, most had but one room, only six of them had a separate byre, and many had dung heaps inside. No vegetables whatsoever were grown save potatoes and cabbage, and no fruit at all. With these deplorable conditions obtaining before the Great Famine struck in 1846, the horror that followed was inevitable.

Despite the awful life they left behind, many of those who managed to emigrate longed for the lonely beauty of the land they had been obliged to leave, while at home, the Ulster life and landscape inspired more fortunate men. At Killybegs in County Donegal in 1849, William Allingham, a descendant of a settler family who arrived there in 1613, wrote his best-known poem, *The Fairies*, which recalls the strong belief that persisted in the "little people":

Up the airy mountain,
Down the rushy glen,
We daren't go a-hunting
For fear of little men;
Wee folk, good folk,
Trooping all together;
Green jacket, red cap,
And white owl's feather!

Down along the rocky shore
Some make their home—
They live on crispy pancakes
Of yellow tide-foam;
Some in the reeds
Of the black mountain lake,
With frogs for their watch-dogs,
All night awake.

High on the hill-top
The old King sits;
He is now so old and grey
He's nigh lost his wits.
With a bridge of white mist
Columbkill he crosses,
On his stately journeys
From Slieveleague to Rosses;
Or going up with music
On cold starry nights,
To sup with the Queen
Of the gay Northern Lights.

They stole little Bridget
For seven years long;
When she came down again
Her friends were all gone.
They took her lightly back,
Between the night and morrow;
They thought that she was fast asleep,
But she was dead with sorrow.
They have kept her ever since
Deep within the lake,
On a bed of flag-leaves,
Watching till she wake.

By the craggy hill-side,
Through the mosses bare,
They have planted thorn-trees
For pleasure here and there.
Is any man so daring
As dig one up in spite,

He shall find their sharpest thorns
In his bed at night.

Ulster folkways also inspired the novelist William Carleton, a native of County Tyrone, to write his *Traits and Stories of the Irish Peasantry* in 1837. In *Adieu to Belashanny*, Allingham eulogized Ballyshannon, County Donegal, his birthplace, its "buoyant salted air," and the "green-hill'd harbour." His poem most evocative of Donegal, however, is *Abbey Asaroe*:

Grey, grey is Abbey Asaroe, by Belashanny town,
It has neither doors nor windows, the walls are broken
    down;
The carven-stones lie scattered in briar and nettle-bed;
The only feet are those that come at burial of the dead.
A little rocky rivulet runs murmuring to the tide,
Singing a song of ancient days, in sorrow, not in pride;
The boortree and the lightsome ash across the portal
    grow,
And heaven itself is now the roof of Abbey Asaroe.

It looks beyond the harbour-stream to Gulban mountain
    blue;
It hears the voice of Erna's fall,—Atlantic breakers too;
High ships go sailing past it; the sturdy clank of oars
Brings in the salmon-boat to haul a net upon the shores;
And this way to his home-creek, when the summer day
    is done,
Slow sculls the weary fisherman across the setting sun;
While green with corn is Sheegus Hill, his cottage white
    below;
But grey at every season is Abbey Asaroe.

There stood one day a poor old man above its broken
    bridge;
He heard no running rivulet, he saw no mountain-ridge;
He turned his back on Sheegus Hill and viewed with
    misty sight
The Abbey walls, the burial-ground with crosses ghostly
    white;
Under a weary weight of years he bowed upon his staff,
Perusing in the present time the former's epitaph;
For, grey and wasted like the walls, a figure full of woe,
This man was of the blood of them who founded
    Asaroe.

From Derry to Bundrowas Tower, Tirconnell broad was
    theirs;
Spearmen and plunder, bards and wine, and holy abbot's
    prayers;
With changing always in the house that they had builded
    high
To God and to Saint Bernard,—where at last they came
    to die.
At worst, no workhouse grave for him! the ruins of his
    race
Shall rest among the ruin'd stones of this their saintly
    place.
The fond old man was weeping; and tremulous and slow
Along the rough and crooked lane he crept from Asaroe.

It was an Ulster poet, William Drennan, a son of the minister of the Rosemary Street Presbyterian Church, Belfast, and an ardent Irish nationalist, who first called Ireland "the Emerald Isle" in a poem written in 1795. Belfast was also the birthplace of the nineteenth-century poet and antiquary, Sir Samuel Ferguson, and of the poet, Louis MacNeice (1907–1963) who, in his autobiography, *The Strings Are False*, recalled his childhood at Carrickfergus, County Antrim, where his father was the rector. Another recent Belfast-born writer, C. S. Lewis, wrote of his childhood in the suburbs of the city, in his autobiography, *Surprised by Joy*. His house, he remembered, "looked down over wide fields to Belfast Lough and across it to the long mountain line of the Antrim shore."

During the famine years, in the comfort of her home, Milltown House in Strabane, County Tyrone, Miss Cecil Frances Humphreys, better known by her married name as Mrs. C. F. Alexander, wrote hymns which are still sung by English-speaking people all over the world; the best known are the Easter hymn, *There is a Green Hill Far Away* and the Christmas carol, *Once in Royal David's City*. Mrs. Alexander's philosophy must have helped to carry her through the Famine and face the drastic plight of the have-nots, for in another of her popular hymns, *All Things Bright and Beautiful*, she wrote with carefree determination a verse which is now prudently omitted from the hymnals:

The rich man in his castle
The poor man at his gate,
God made them high or lowly
And ordered their estate.

The local authorities responsible for choosing or registering street names in Ulster towns do not seem to have consulted the poets. The people have now just won a battle with the Post Office to retain their old townland names. But, who were the humorless men who named Flush Place in Lurgan and Flush Gardens in Belfast, or Belfast's Waterproof Street, Laundry Avenue, and Chlorine Gardens? The farflung outposts of the British Empire inspired a number of Belfast streets like Baroda Parade, Kashmir Street, and Bombay Street. But the people in these streets had their own poets. Was it in Eureka Street or Crimea Street that the children used to sing, "Our Queen can birl her leg, birl her leg, birl her leg, Our Queen can birl her leg, birl her leg..."? This is only one of the many popular Belfast street songs, urban folk creations which are a treasury of humor, often gaily ribald:

You might easy know a doffer
When she comes into town
With her long yella' hair
And her pickers hangin' down.

In recent times Ulster has produced several notable writers, among them George William Russell (1867–1935), the poet and artist, better known as AE, who was born in Lurgan, County Armagh; the novelist and journalist Benedict Kiely and the poet John Montague (born 1929), both from County Tyrone; the poet Patrick Kavanagh (1904–1967), whose poem *Shancoduff* immortalized the hills around his farm at Inniskeen, County Monaghan:

My black hills have never seen the sun rising,
Eternally they look north towards Armagh,
Lot's wife would not be salt if she had been
Incurious as my black hills that are happy
When dawn whitens Glassdrummond Chapel.

My hills hoard the bright shillings of March
While the sun searches in every pocket.
They are my Alps and I have climbed the Matterhorn
With a sheaf of hay for three perishing calves
In the field under the Big Forth of Rocksavage.

The sleety winds fondle the rushy beards of Shancoduff
While the cattle-drovers sheltering in the Featherna
    Bush

Look up and say: "Who owns them hungry hills
That the water-hen and snipe must have forsaken?
A poet? Then by heavens he must be poor."
I hear and is my heart not badly shaken?

Kavanagh's *The Great Hunger* is a cry against the frustrations of rural life, and his *Spraying the Potatoes*, a sensuous lyrical memory of a simple rural episode.

John Montague is the senior of a generation of excellent contemporary poets from Ulster of whom the best known are James Simmons (born in 1933), Seamus Heaney and Michael Longley (both born in 1939), Derek Mahon (born in 1941) and Paul Muldoon (born in 1951), and Belfast can boast of a flourishing band of working-class poets.

Although the contemporary Ulster writers have not chosen the land particularly as their theme, it is not surprising that poets and painters should spring from the contrasts of urban Ulster with the beautiful countryside: the magnificence of Fair Head, a bastion of the Antrim Plateau, the Giant's Causeway, one of the world's most scenic land forms, the heather-clad crags of the Devil's Backbone mirrored in the shining waters of Lough Swilly, or the forest of Glenveagh, the home of the largest herd of red deer in Ireland.

Ulster has thirty-one National Nature Reserves as well as Forest Nature Reserves and bird sanctuaries, and a splendid variety of wild life. Badger, otter, fox, and hare make their home in the province, and there are mountain goats clambering in the unspoiled glens of the Braid Valley, which runs from near Ballymena into the Antrim moorlands. After some decades of absence the rare golden eagle now soars again over the peaks of County Donegal. Thousands of seabirds make their home on Rathlin Island, which now has only one hundred inhabitants and where the last Irish speaker died within living memory. It is a great place for deep-sea fishing, for trapping lobster or for catching conger eels in the underwater wreckage of unlucky ships. Puffins, kittiwakes, guillemots, razorbills, and cormorants perch on the rocks of Rathlin, and buzzards make their nests there.

Grebe nest around Lough Erne in County Fermanagh, while only a few miles from the tension and hubbub of busy Belfast is Strangford Lough, a stopping place between the Arctic and the tropics for thousands of migrant birds. It is the wintering place for thousands of wild geese. The Lough, which abounds with fish including the giant skate,

is also the home of golden plover and of around one
hundred thousand waders as well as oystercatchers, godwit
and curlew.

And of the many small creatures of the countryside the
Ulster poet Paul Muldoon has not let us forget the
hedgehog, in his poem which also expresses that
underlying sadness of his province:

> The snail moves like a
> Hovercraft, held up by a
> Rubber cushion of itself,
> Sharing its secret
>
> With the hedgehog. The hedgehog
> Shares its secret with no one.

> We say, Hedgehog, come out
> Of yourself and we will love you.
>
> We mean no harm. We want
> Only to listen to what
> You have to say. We want
> Your answers to our questions.
>
> The hedgehog gives nothing
> Away, keeping itself to itself.
> We wonder what a hedgehog
> Has to hide, why it so distrusts.
>
> We forget the god
> Under this crown of thorns.
> We forget that never again
> Will a god trust in the world.

Swans on the shore of Mulroy Bay, County Donegal.

opposite: *The edge of the lake from the former garden of Quilca House, County Cavan, where Dean Swift stayed with the Sheridan family and wrote much of* Gulliver's Travels. *The Dean remembered in verse the discomfort he and Stella endured at Quilca.*

above: Caltha palustris, *commonly known as marsh marigolds or kingcups, growing on the edge of the lake at Quilca.*

above: *The fine beaches of the narrow Rosguill Peninsula, County Donegal, now a popular seaside resort.*

left: *Duck-shooting stage, Boa Island, Lough Erne, County Fermanagh.*

opposite: *One of the most important scenic landforms in the world, the majestic rock formation of the Giant's Causeway on the northern coast of County Antrim, a unique part of Ireland's geological heritage. In the course of Tertiary igneous activity, the lowest layer of lava cooled slowly and with a uniform pattern of contraction, thus creating thousands of hexagonal columns, some of which have been isolated by weathering.*

above: *"Giant's Eyes," Giant's Causeway.*

below: *In the Tertiary Period, about fifty million years ago, tropical weathering of the basalt led to a concentration of iron and aluminum hydroxides. A bright orange-red streak of the interbasaltic bed separates the lower and middle basalts in the cliffs of the Giant's Causeway.*

following spread: *Fishing boats, Downings Pier, County Donegal.*

49

above: *Vestiges of innocent paganism cling to many celebrated Christian holy places in Ireland. This holy well just south of the Rock of Doon, County Donegal, the ancient inauguration place of the O'Donnell chiefs, has been visited by pilgrims for centuries. Here, those seeking cures tie pieces of a garment to branches placed near the well. Medicine bottles, empty suppository boxes, crutches, coins, rosaries, empty wine bottles, combs, handkerchiefs, and bits of clothing are left lying about as reminders of a healing desired or ex-votos for a healing obtained.*

opposite: *A Ballycastle skipper and his men haul in lobster pots off Fair Head, County Antrim. Most of the catch goes to the Continent, especially France, where it commands a good price.*

opposite: *Seabirds, Rathlin Island, County Antrim. In rough weather, the crossing from the mainland to Rathlin can be dangerous, and many ships have been wrecked there.*

below: *Cormorants on a rock off Rathlin Island.*

above: *Stormont, Belfast, was built between 1928 and 1932 following the division of Ireland to house the Parliament of Northern Ireland. For Ulster Loyalists it is the symbol of law and order and of their attachment to the British Crown; for Nationalists it represents a government that is partisan and corrupt.*

opposite: *View of farmlands from the top of the keep of Dundrum Castle, County Down.*

A view of Armagh from the steps of the Roman Catholic cathedral. The statue of Archbishop Daniel McGettigan looks across to the Protestant cathedral on a neighboring hill.

*A farmer makes tea over a turf fire on the
bog near Glenveagh, County Donegal.*

above: *Wild goat in Braid Valley, County Antrim.*

below: *Ewe in the Mourne Mountains, County Down.*

following spread:

Detail of the south transept of St. Macartan's Cathedral, County Monaghan, begun in 1861. Saint Dympna is flanked by two nineteenth-century bishops, an ancient soldier-bishop, and three Irish saints.

far right, top to bottom: *Friars of the Order of Saint Francis, which established houses in Ireland in the Middle Ages. After the dissolution of the monasteries the Friars held on tenaciously. During the prohibitions of penal times they lived in disguise among the people, continuing their ministry and keeping the old faith alive.*

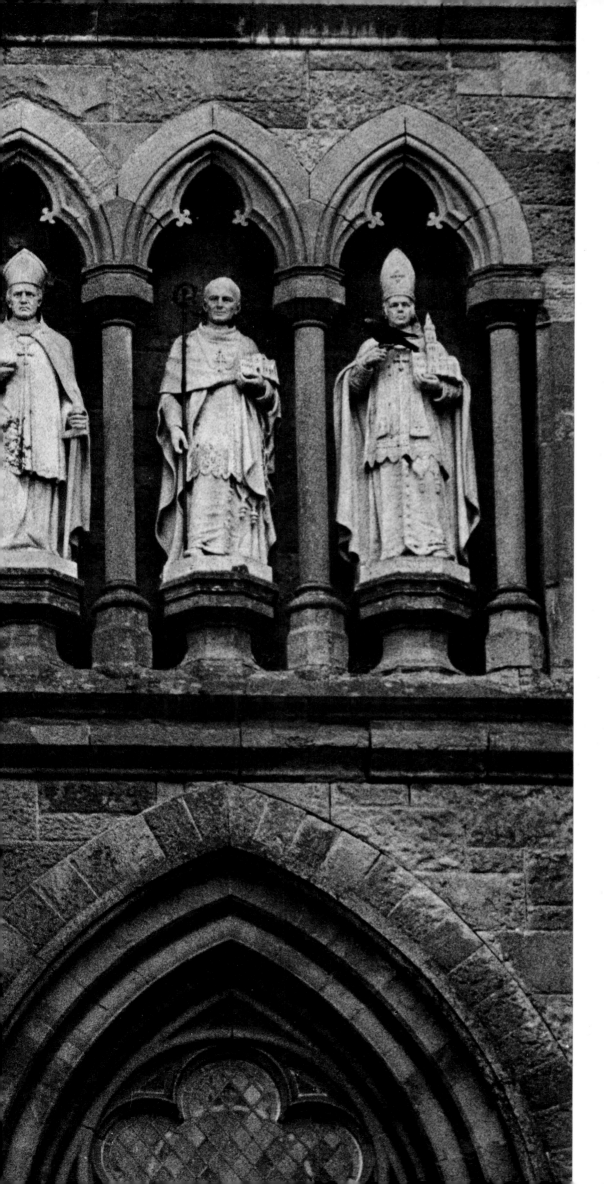

opposite: *Evening at Glen Head, Glencolumbkille, County Donegal.*

below: *The keep of Dundrum Castle, County Down.*

following spread: *On the hill of Dundrum, County Down, at the lower edge of the lower ward of the Norman castle, is the shell of a seventeenth-century gabled mansion, built by the Blundell family.*

opposite: *A donkey looks over the cyclopean stonework of a wall on Cruit Island, beyond Gweedore, County Donegal.*

above and below: *Visual reminders of partition: rural telephone booths in Ulster have different colors, take different coinage, are named in different languages. The green telefón is in the Republic at Doagh, County Donegal; the British red telephone, at Leggs on Lough Erne, County Fermanagh.*

Leinster

"In a quiet water'd land"

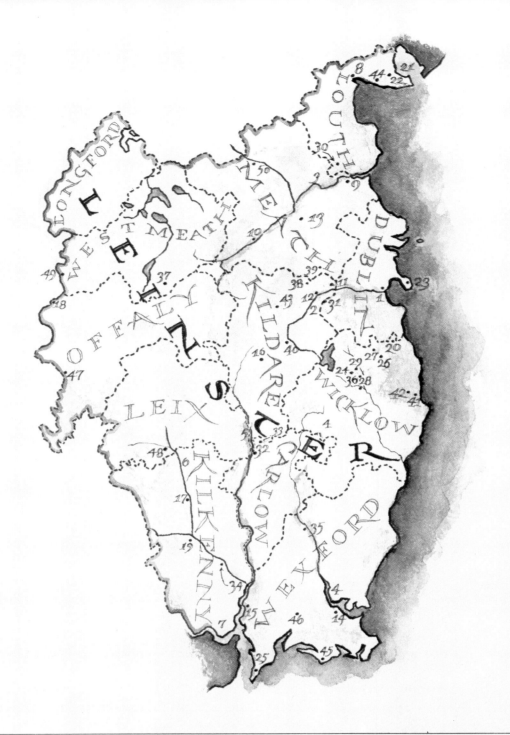

1	Dublin	18	Clonmacnoise	35	Ballycarney
2	River Liffey	19	Jerpoint Abbey	36	Laragh
3	River Boyne	20	Powerscourt	37	Tyrrelspass
4	River Slaney	21	Carlingford Lough	38	Maynooth
5	River Barrow	22	Cooley Peninsula	39	Dunboyne
6	River Nore	23	Howth	40	Bannockstown
7	River Suir	24	Glendalough	41	Wicklow
8	Dundalk	25	Hook Head	42	Mount Usher
9	Drogheda	26	Luggala	43	Robertstown
10	Trim	27	Sallygap	44	Faughart
11	Leixlip	28	Glenmalure	45	Kilmore Quay
12	Celbridge	29	Glenmacnass	46	Foulkesmill
13	Tara	30	Monasterboice	47	Birr
14	Wexford	31	Newcastle	48	Durrow
15	Dunbrody Abbey	32	Carlow	49	Athlone
16	The Curragh	33	Browneshill	50	Kells
17	Kilkenny	34	Inistioge		

preceding spread: *Tyrrelspass, County Westmeath, one of the most elegant villages in Leinster, is a legacy of landlord improvement by the Rochforts, Earls of Belvedere, who favored a formal layout around a semicircular green. The Rochforts established a savings bank, a charitable loan fund, a dispensary, churches, and schools. The town is now lovingly cared for by its inhabitants.*

L einster is the most prosperous and the most progressive province, because it has long been open to outside influence. Since it contains the capital of the Republic , and since a disproportionately high percentage of the population of Ireland is concentrated in Dublin City and County, Leinster is the most cosmopolitan of Ireland's four provinces. Certainly it is the one whose population has the greatest ethnic mixture in its ancestry.

The population of County Dublin is now approaching one million, about one-third of the entire population of the Republic. While the population of the country as a whole diminished dramatically, that of Dublin City steadily increased; between 1841 and 1971 it more than doubled from 232,726 to 566,034, while over the same period the population of Ireland dropped from over eight million to four and a half million, of whom one and a half million are in the six counties of Northern Ireland. Because of this population movement the proportion of the population of the whole island residing in Dublin rose from one in thirty-two in 1841 to one in eight in 1971, while if only the twenty-six counties are considered, the ratio residing in the capital is one in five. The radical change is even more remarkable in the growth of Dun Laoghaire only eight miles south of Dublin City, which developed in the nineteenth century as Kingstown, a small urban nucleus around the harbor. Between 1841 and 1971 the population of Dun Laoghaire rose by 1300 percent to make it one of only four towns in the Republic with a population of over fifty thousand. This shift in population towards Dublin commenced in the five years immediately following the Famine when the population of every county in Ireland, except Dublin, dropped by at least 11 percent, and in one county as much as 31 percent, due to death and emigration, while the population of County Dublin actually increased by 9 percent.

Other coastal towns of Leinster have grown, although less dramatically than Dun Laoghaire. Between 1841 and 1971 the population of Dundalk, County Louth, increased by 121 percent, of Drogheda, County Louth, by 24 percent, of Bray, County Wicklow, by 400 percent, of Arklow, County Wicklow, by 116 percent, of Wexford by 18 percent, while the population of Kilkenny, an important town in the interior, decreased by 35 percent. Leinster's long coastline, stretching from Carlingford Bay to the north, to Hook Head, the eastern extremity of Waterford Harbour, in the southeast, combined with this concentration of population in the coastal towns, gives an impression of Leinster as a maritime province, but this is not so. Eight of the province's twelve counties, Kildare, Meath, Westmeath, Longford, Carlow, Kilkenny, Leix and Offaly are landlocked, and only four, Louth, Dublin, Wicklow and Wexford, have a seaboard.

The census returns reveal other figures that bear on the personality of Leinster. Already in 1841, of all the counties, County Dublin had much the lowest percentage of its population engaged in agriculture, only 32 percent, while the national average was 67 percent and the average for the province of Leinster was 62.5 percent. Before the Famine and the slow growth of industry, when the textile industry flourished mainly in Ulster, there was already textile production in Leinster at Collon and Drogheda in County Louth; Navan, County Meath; Balbriggan, and Dublin City in County Dublin; Stratford-on-the-Slaney in County Wicklow; Mountmellick and Abbeyleix in County Leix; and at Kilkenny. There were distilleries at Dundalk, County Louth, Dublin City, Monasterevin, County Kildare, and at Birr and Tullamore in County Offaly. Dublin and Drogheda also already had breweries, and at Dundalk, Drogheda and Dublin there were corn-mills of some importance. Linen was exported from the port of Dublin, where the bulk of the country's import of tea arrived; corn, meal and flour were the main exports from Dundalk, Drogheda and Wexford, which specialized in the import of coal, tobacco, and woollen manufactures respectively. In 1841, 66 percent of the population of Dublin was literate against the national average of only 48 percent; the average for Leinster was 53.6 percent.

Leinster's commercial activity and external links can be traced back over one thousand years to the trading activities of the Vikings. The monastic orders from France that came in the twelfth century forged further links with the Continent; the Cistercians introduced their system of marketing their produce, which was a stimulus to commercial activity. The technically advanced Anglo-Norman invaders arrived at the end of the twelfth century. They gave Dublin its legal status, made it their capital, and moving into the Leinster hinterland, gave it the man-made appearance it reveals today, leaving the impress of their program of settlement on much of the province. Norman consolidation was effected overwhelmingly in Leinster where the majority of their mottes and castles can be found, and four out of nine of their early walled towns in the country, Drogheda, Dublin, Wexford, and New Ross. By the end of the thirteenth century settlers had come from England in considerable numbers in the wake of the Norman barons and knights. They settled mostly in the eastern counties, but the biggest concentration was in the Anglo-Norman Pale, which until the Tudor expansion was an area from Dublin to Drogheda with some of the Meath and Kildare hinterland, where the jurisdiction of the

Crown's authority was truly effective. This region in particular was subjected to centuries of anglicization. By the end of the sixteenth century the Crown managed to extend the boundary of the Pale to include nine of the present twelve counties of Leinster, thus further accentuating the difference between Leinster and the rest of the country.

The building and rebuilding under the Viceroy Ormonde after the Restoration in 1660 speeded the development of Dublin, and in the eighteenth century the capital was the scene of a veritable boom. The great landowners built themselves mansions in the metropolis, and magnates, who also usually held a seat in Parliament, erected great country houses and elegant villas within reasonable access of the capital, among them Speaker Conolly's magnificent Castletown at Celbridge, Speaker Ponsonby's Bishopscourt, and Lucan House built by Agmondisham Vesey M.P., all in County Kildare; Speaker Foster's Oriel Temple in County Louth; Russborough, built by Joseph Leeson M.P., later 1st Earl of Milltown, and Powerscourt, built by Richard Wingfield M.P., later 1st Viscount Powerscourt, both in County Wicklow. Nathaniel Clements M.P. built his Palladianesque villa just outside the city in the Royal Deer Park, now Phoenix Park. This house later became the Viceregal Lodge, and now with additions, is the official residence of the President of Ireland.

The privileged situation of Leinster is clear from the glaringly uneven representation of members in the Irish parliament prior to the Union in 1800. Leinster returned 132 members against Ulster's 76, Munster's 62, and Connacht's 30. County Wexford alone was represented by 18 members, County Kilkenny by 16, and County Meath by 14. Now, the 144 members of Dail Eireann are elected by adult suffrage and proportional representation, so Leinster, because of its greater population, still has the highest representation in the government. Each of the Republic's 144 electoral constituencies is geared to represent about twenty thousand electors; Leinster has 68 constituencies, almost half of the total for the Republic, and Dublin City and County have 37 constituencies, about a quarter of the state's total.

In prehistoric times neolithic man was attracted to the Boyne Valley, about fifteen kilometers from the east coast and fifty from Dublin, where a strong concentration of passage graves survives, an astonishing witness to the presence, the activities, the faith, the technical skill, and the nonrepresentational art of the builders. Radiocarbon tests on undisturbed material in the passage roof at Newgrange, Ireland's most impressive Stone Age monument, gave dates centering on 2500 B.C. There is scant evidence of inhabitation of this region by the earlier mesolithic

fisher-and-fowler folk but a large labor force must have been available to the immigrant passage grave builders. Either the older inhabitants were already there without leaving much trace, or they migrated to the area from farther north and joined the passage grave settlements when the new people came to the valley. In his *Prehistoric Elements in our Heritage*, the author, H. J. Fleure, sees these extraordinary monuments not as an isolated achievement of a vanished people, but as a vital contribution to western European heritage.

George Coffey made a remarkable study of the Boyne graves at the end of the last century. With extraordinary acumen he saw in them the beginnings of decorative art in Ireland, and recognized both the possibility of a symbolic meaning of some of the figures and also their use only as ornamentation. Coffey's findings are more satisfactory than those of later researchers, who endeavored to discern anthropomorphic or representational elements in the motifs and to classify them accordingly. Many of these researchers made a determined effort to find in the Boyne Valley passage grave decoration the influence of the art of Iberian and Breton passage graves and of anthropomorphic idols, plaques and amulets found in Iberian tombs. However, the affinities are tenuous and now the dating of Newgrange makes such a derivation most unlikely. It is also significant that the spiral, which was a favored motif in Ireland, is only found at one isolated site on the continent, Gavrinis.

The majority of the slabs were decorated before positioning. The designs were mostly made on the natural surface of stone by pitting or picking with a sharp tool, perhaps a flint or a piece of quartz, and the designs are often as clear today as when they were made. The motifs range from circles (the most common figure), spirals, serpentiforms, arcs, lozenges, zigzags, parallels and radials, to amorphous doodles. The variety and inequality of this range has led Claire O'Kelly to conclude in her *Passage-grave Art in the Boyne Valley* that the actual carving of the stones was an important element of the cult, fulfilling a ritual, spiritual, or symbolic function, but less integral to the cult generally than the placing of objects such as stone beads, chalk marbles, and pendants in the tomb chambers.

The builders of Newgrange were far from being stupid cave dwellers living in primitive ignorance. Their intellectual sophistication has been proved by an experiment carried out in 1969 by Professor M. J. O'Kelly. Until that time it had been thought that a sort of roof box in the passage must have been constructed as a repository from which offerings, such as food for the dead person's sustenance in the other world, could be dropped through a gap in the capstones. Professor O'Kelly's experiment showed that the tomb itself and its passage had been carefully and precisely oriented so that a straight line led from the back of the tomb to the center of the roof box in alignment with the spot on the horizon where the sun rises on the shortest day of the year, Midwinter's Day. On December 21, 1969, Professor O'Kelly waited in the tomb chamber for the sun to rise and then witnessed how a slender beam of sunlight penetrated the chamber through the roof box and the gap in the capstones, and shone on the hindmost burial niche for seventeen minutes. This can only occur on Midwinter's Day and the days immediately preceding and following it.

The gallery grave builders were also active in Leinster, and the portal grave builders have left evidence of their presence in the eastern part of the province, from the dolmen known as Leac An Scail at Kilmogue, County Kilkenny, in the south, to the dolmen at Proleek, near Ballymascanlon, County Louth, in the north. The Browneshill dolmen near the town of Carlow is reputed to have the heaviest capstone of any in Europe, a gigantic granite erratic block; the Haroldstown dolmen in the same county has two capstones supported by ten stones. At Brennanstown, County Dublin, there is a fine example in which the chamber is formed by seven stones supporting a large capstone; the dolmen at Kilternan, also in County Dublin, has an even more impressive capstone and there are other dolmens in the county at Larch Hill and Mount Venus; and one in the gardens of Howth Castle, known as Aideen's Grave, was commemorated in a poem of that title by the nineteenth-century poet and antiquary Sir Samuel Ferguson. The most northerly dolmen in Leinster, at Proleek in County Louth, in the same field as the remains of a wedge-shaped gallery grave, has a capstone, weighing about forty thousand kilos, supported by three great stones.

Several of the Iron Age hill forts were important Celtic places of assembly. Tara in County Meath, the best known, was the seat of the pagan priest-kings who were at the zenith of their power when Saint Patrick came there. Teltown, also in County Meath, associated with the goddess Tailtu, was the site of a summer assembly of the men of Ireland where the midpoint of the grazing season and the beginning of the harvest were celebrated. Ushnagh, in County Westmeath where the five ancient provinces of Ireland converged, was the place of the May Day assembly, and the Hill of Ward in County Meath, associated with the Celtic god Lug and dedicated to the cult of a sacred fire, was the meeting place on the first day of winter.

There is evidence on the sites of some of the Leinster hill forts of their earlier use in the Bronze Age, particularly at Baltinglass Hill, County Wicklow, and on the Hill of Tara, where Bronze Age passage grave burial mounds have been excavated, and at Dun Ailinne in County Kildare, the ancient seat of the Kings of Leinster. Tests on samples from the fill of a ditch beneath the cairn of a passage grave on the Mound of the Hostages at Tara gave dates centering on 2100 B.C., long before the construction of the hill fort and the period of Tara's preeminence as a royal and sacred place. It must be concluded therefore that the newcomers deliberately occupied sites already selected.

The Hill of Tara is a disappointing place now and surely it must be difficult for even the most imaginative visitor to picture the glory which seems to have existed even before the Celts and which persisted long after the conversion of the Irish to Christianity, when the claimants to an often ephemeral, and until Brian Ború, an invariably nominal High Kingship, were inaugurated there on the stone *Lia Fáil*. There is no vestige of the great royal banqueting hall where seats were assigned strictly according to rank; a long hollow area surrounded by banks may have been where it stood, but like the other buildings of the palace constructed of perishable materials like daub, wattle and wood, it has vanished. According to protocol, the royal family and nobles at the top of the table feasted on ribs of beef, the druids, soothsayers and chess players on the shins, and the historians on the haunches. The musicians' fare was shoulder of pork, while the poor jesters ate shoulder fat. The disappearance of archeological remains at Tara throughout the latter half of the nineteenth century was then accelerated by a group of British Israelites, who demolished with lunatic fervor a mound that Petrie had seen in an effort to find the Ark of the Covenant, which one of their number had seen buried there in a dream. No Ark was found and a considerable area of the ancient site was devastated.

It seems that when Saint Patrick and a small party of followers sailed up the Boyne and ascended the Hill of Slane to celebrate Easter, the pagan court on the summit of Tara may have been about to celebrate a cult ritual involving lighting a sacred fire. However, before their fire was lit, Patrick had his Paschal fire blazing nine miles away on the Hill of Slane. As it was forbidden to light a fire before the royal fire was ignited, the King and his druids, who were incensed at the breach of protocol, set out for Slane in nine chariots to investigate.

On the green Hill of Slane they were met by Patrick, who explained the symbolism of his Paschal fire and preached the divinity of Christ. According to Patrick's biographer, a druid, seeing that Patrick's message made an impression on some of the royal party, uttered a blasphemy to counteract the effect. Saint Patrick immediately caused the druid to be miraculously raised high in the air where, presumably, he turned a half somersault, because he dashed out his brains on a stone when he reached the ground again. The King ordered his guards to seize Patrick, but the saint cried out with a loud voice *"Exurgat Deus"* and the King's men were thrown into confusion and started to fight among themselves; the horses bolted, smashing the chariots in their wild career. Only the King, his wife, and two attendants were left of the Royal party. The Queen interceded with the Saint not to kill her husband, promising that he would be converted.

On the next day, an Easter Sunday that coincided with the Vernal Equinox, Patrick visited the court at Tara, entering the banquet hall with five followers, although the doors were closed. The King invited Patrick to join the feast, but while Patrick was saying grace, a druid took the opportunity to pour some handy poison into the Saint's cup. By a miracle the beverage in the cup froze while the poison remained liquid; after pouring it away Patrick blessed the cup and then the frozen, uncontaminated beverage melted. The frustrated druid proposed a contest of miracle-working, and for his first feat covered the ground with a thick mantle of snow. Patrick recited a blessing and the snow disappeared. The druid then called down darkness to shroud the place. Patrick dismissed it and brought back the sunlight. The King then proposed that both the druid and Patrick should plunge their books into water and that he would worship the party whose books came out undamaged. However, the druid refused this trial and a similar one in fire. Finally, Patrick handed his cloak to the druid and proposed that he should put it on and go into a hut built half of green and half of dry wood, together with Patrick's youthful follower Benignus, who would wear the druid's gown, and that the hut should be set on fire. The druid, embarrassed before the assembly, agreed. The fire consumed the green wood and the druid, but not the Saint's cloak, which he had worn; the dry wood did not ignite, and Benignus came out unscathed, although the druid's gown, which he had worn, had been consumed.

The Irish Early Christian world after the conversion of the monarchs and the people was an unique one in which pre-Celtic and Celtic traditions and ethics mingled with the new moral and spiritual code. Professor E. Estyn Evans, in his *The Personality of Ireland,* has written aptly of this assimilation: "The enduring success of Christianity in its conquest of Ireland was due to conscious and unconscious syncretism and its adjustment to the personality of Ireland: in fact it might be said with some truth that Ireland conquered Christianity. Hence once more we see the power of the native tradition to assimilate new elements and to transmute them into something distinctly Irish."

Descriptions of life and customs in Early Christian Ireland that can be garnered from reliable sources range from the inspirational to the curious, the startling and the hair-raising. It is clear from the sixth-century Penitential of Finnian that divorce and concubinage were common, that slave-owning was tolerated, that many priests were married, and that priests were inclined to indulge in pre-Christian magic such as preparing potions. But what is one to make of the Christian women of Ireland of whom the good seventh-century Abbot Adamnán wrote in his *Cáin Adamnáin* (The Law of Adamnán) that "Even the best of women had to go into battle and battlefield, camping and fighting, wounding and slaying, her bag of food on one side, her babe on the other, and with her a wooden pole and an iron hook on the end. Her husband was behind her, carrying the stake of a fence, and flogging her to battle. And she would fix her hook in the tresses of women on the opposite side, for at that time women's heads were the chief battle trophies."

There was certainly room for reform at all levels, from the laity to the hierarchy, and especially among the powerful abbots whose office was often hereditary. In his *Life of Columcille,* Adamnán recounts the incident of Aedh Dubh, a young prince, who after a life of violence entered a monastery and undertook a pilgrimage; however, when his abbot, Findchán, presented him to the bishop for ordination to the priesthood, the bishop was loathe to perform the ceremony. He doubted the candidate's suitability and considered that the abbot had not recognized this because he was blinded by his carnal infatuation (*carnaliter amans*) and therefore unable to exercise his discernment. But the bishop was not powerful enough to refuse the abbot's request, so he agreed to ordain Aedh if the abbot laid his right hand on the young man's head too, for confirmation. It is clear also from Brian Ború's plural marriages for example, that by this time the Church had still not managed to impose its code and its canon law. In a secular tract, *Bretha Crólige, Ériu,* a lawyer attempted to justify arguments in favor of the polygamy practiced by the Christian Irish by citing the examples of the Old Testament: "There is a dispute in Irish Law as to which is more proper, whether many sexual unions or a single one: for the chosen people of God lived in plurality of unions so that it is not easier to condemn it than to praise it."

John V. Kelleher has translated from the Irish an epigram which reveals what may have been a prevalent Irish attitude to doctrine, reform and salvation:

Cú Chuimne in youth
Read his way through half the truth.
He let the other half lie
While he gave women a try.

Well for him in old age.
He became a holy sage.
He gave women the laugh.
He read the other half.

At the other end of the spectrum were the ascetic monks deeply attached to their devotional life and expert at the decorative arts, particularly manuscript work. Talented artisans of the period made exquisite brooches, pins, altar vessels and reliquaries. Beautiful ornamental metalwork was produced, mostly of bronze, sometimes tinned, or of silver, sometimes gilded. Some of the most renowned artifacts are associated with Leinster. The exquisitely detailed Tara Brooch was found with other objects, probably abandoned loot, near the mouth of the River Boyne; it is of silver with panels of very fine gold filigree work. The supreme achievement of Celtic Christian art is known as the *Book of Kells,* after the monastery of Saint Columcille at Kells in County Meath where it was kept until 1007, and where these illuminated gospels may have been executed. There was certainly an important workshop at Kells where the Cathach of Columcille was sent to be enshrined, and another important workshop was attached to the great monastery at Clonmacnoise in County Offaly. The *Book of Durrow,* a beautiful illuminated gospel, was produced in an Irish scriptorium, most likely of the monastery at Durrow in County Leix. Millefiori and other glass objects have been found on the royal site at Lagore, County Meath, where there was a glassworks.

Leinster has many important monastic sites. County Wicklow has Glendalough, a superb site enfolded in a deep glen between mountains where Saint Kevin founded a community in the sixth century. According to the legend, Kevin retired to this spot to be alone because his good looks made him a source of temptation. He was obliged to drown one persistent lady who followed him to his lonely bed and made vigorous attempts to share it. Another story relates that he dealt with a young woman who pursued him by stripping and rolling in nettles to mortify his own flesh, then beating her in the face with nettles until she was purged of desire. She became a nun. Whatever the truth of these tales, Saint Kevin's monastery flourished and attracted great numbers of students, even from abroad.

Saint Bede, the Anglo-Saxon theologian and historian, wrote of Glendalough in the eighth century: "Many of the nobles of the English nation and lesser men also had set out thither, forsaking their native island either for grace of sacred teaching or a more austere life. And some of them indeed soon dedicated themselves faithfully to the monastic life, others rejoiced rather to give themselves to learning, going about from one master's cell to another. All these the Irish willingly received, and saw to it to supply them with food day by day without cost, and books for their studies, and teaching, free of charge."

Saint Mullin's monastery in County Carlow, founded in the seventh century by Saint Moling, has been called a miniature Glendalough; it was the burial place of the Kings of South Leinster. A seventh-century manuscript, the *Book of Mulling,* contains an early plan of this monastery. There are no remains of the once-great monastery at Clonard in County Meath. Of Saint Columcille's famous foundation at Kells in the same county, only a Round Tower survives on the top of the hill, some High Crosses, and a single-cell stone church with a steeply pitched roof. Among the remains at Monasterboice, County Louth, where the monastery was founded in the sixth century, is the Cross of Muiredach, one of the most perfect High Crosses in the country. Only a small stone church is left of Saint Fechin's seventh-century foundation at Fore in County Westmeath where there once were three hundred monks.

There was another important monastery at Durrow in what is now County Leix, founded by Saint Columcille, and two in what is now County Offaly: Seirkieran, associated with Saint Kieran the elder, a contemporary of Saint Patrick, and Clonmacnoise, "greater than kingdoms in its dignity," founded in the sixth century by another Saint Kieran who is recorded as belonging to a family of pre-Celtic origin living in County Meath, where the Saint made his novitiate under Saint Finnian at Clonard. Kieran's own foundation on the eastern bank of the Shannon at Clonmacnoise grew rapidly, although the founder himself in early middle age succumbed to the plague. His monastery became one of the most celebrated—perhaps the most celebrated monastery in Ireland. Clonmacnoise is not a bridging point across the Shannon because of lack of firm ground on the Connacht bank; the pilgrim's road ran along the adjoining esker with a crossing at Shannonbridge, where eskers on both sides of the river provide firm ground for a bridge. The monastery was patronized by the great families of Connacht across the river, among them the MacDermots and the O'Conors; Rory O'Conor, King of Connacht and last High King of Ireland, who died in 1198, was buried at Clonmacnoise, as was his father King Tirlogh. The monastery was a great center of learning and of the arts; in its scriptorium were produced *The Annals of Tighernach* and the *Book of the Dun Cow.*

A number of intricately carved and decorated grave slabs have survived, evidence of the monastery's popularity and importance as a burial place. Thomas William Rolleston (1857-1920), himself a native of County Offaly, commemorated the illustrious patrons who were buried there in *The Dead at Clonmacnoise*. These verses of Rolleston's are from his freely romantic translation and adaptation of the poet O'Gillan's original Irish:

In a quiet water'd land, a land of roses
Stands Saint Kieran's city fair;
And the warriors of Erin in their famous generations
    Slumber there.
There beneath the dewy hillside sleep the noblest
    Of the clan of Conn,
Each below his stone with name in branching Ogham
    And the sacred knot thereon.

Picturesquely scattered above the gentle curves of the Shannon are the remains of the once-great monastic establishment. The Vikings, coming up the Shannon, attacked Clonmacnoise at least eight times; on one of those occasions the Norse chief set his wife Ota up on the high altar to pronounce oracles. The Irish themselves attacked and pillaged the monastery, sometimes in the internecine clan struggles, sometimes in skirmishes with a rival monastery. In the twelfth century the Anglo-Normans in their westward advance attacked Clonmacnoise, and in 1552 it was raided and partly demolished by the English forces from Athlone, who looted the treasury. In the 1640s an attempt to restore at least the Cathedral was undone by Cromwellian troopers. Nevertheless there are the remains of seven small churches (one of which, Temple Conor, is still in use for Church of Ireland services), the Cathedral, the Round Tower, and High Crosses. Outside the old enclosure are the ruins of the beautiful twelfth-century Romanesque Nuns' Church built by Derbhorgaill (Dervorguila), Queen of Breffny, whose abduction by Dermot, King of Leinster, led indirectly to the invasion of the Anglo-Norman mercenaries which ended in the takeover of Ireland by the English Crown.

Of the original tenth-century structure of the Cathedral, the antae have survived. The building was repaired in 1080 and 1104, again extensively in 1330, and again in 1460 when Dean Odo inserted the handsome medieval north doorway. The Cross of the Scriptures in front of the Cathedral was sculpted early in the tenth century with didactic scenes from the Bible, the life of Saint Kieran, and phases in the plan of salvation.

Until the discovery of the American continent and the vast migratory wave from Europe to North and South America, no people roved so widely as the Viking farmers, fishermen, and merchant-seamen. Expert seafarers and redoubtable warriors, they sailed from Norway in their cleverly designed ships to the Shetland, Orkney, and Faroe islands and to Iceland. From these islands they moved on to Scotland, the Hebrides, northwestern Britain, the Isle of Man, Ireland, and as far as Greenland. From Denmark they came to eastern Britain and northern France; from the duchy of Normandy, which they established there, groups reached southern Italy and Sicily early in the eleventh century. From Sweden, the Vikings moved eastwards to southern and eastern Finland and the region around Leningrad, then penetrating the interior of Poland and Russia along the inland waterways, they reached the Byzantine Empire and the Baghdad Caliphate.

The first recorded Viking landing in Ireland took place in 795 when they raided Lambay Island, just off the Leinster coast near Dublin. Sporadic raids continuing through the ninth century reached a peak of intensity between 830 and 880. Knowing how to navigate rivers and lakes, the Vikings were able to take full advantage of the opportunities that their new environment provided them. In Ireland they put down roots, and Dublin became one of their most important trading centers.

Since the purpose of the first invaders was to snatch tradeable goods and human slaves, and since the churches and monasteries were the repositories of valuable treasure, they bore the brunt of the forays. The coastal areas were particularly vulnerable. In 821 the Annals record that at Howth "a great prey of women" was taken by the Norsemen. In 837 the Vikings brought their fleets into the Boyne and the Liffey, and in 840, according to the Annals, they captured bishops, priests, and scholars at Louth and took them off as slaves.

The tall, slender cylindrical steeples, called Round Towers, which were built beside a number of Irish churches and monastic establishments and which are a unique feature of the Irish landscape, appear to have been built as bell towers. Their old name in Irish was in fact *cloigtheach*, (bell house), but they were eminently useful as lookouts and places of shelter. The watchman at the top of the tower could ring a warning bell when he saw raiders approaching and the monks could carry their valuables into the tower and withdraw the rope ladder from the entrance, which was usually at least three meters above the ground. It appears that the earliest Round Towers were built about 900 after the heavy spate of systematic Norse raids and in time for the arrival of a great Viking fleet at Waterford in 914. John

Montague has translated a short contemporary verse, *The Vikings,* which expresses the feelings of the people who were subject to the raids:

Bitter the wind tonight,
Combing the sea's hair white:
From the North, no need to fear
The proud sea-coursing warrior.

The Irish had made raids on ecclesiastical property before the Vikings ever came to Ireland and powerful abbots were known to demand their tithe of the spoils from cattle raids. But it seems that as a result of the Viking incursions, the respect of the Irish for sacred places was seriously eroded, and the Annals record numerous raids on churches and monasteries by the Irish from the end of the tenth century, and sometimes raids by combined parties of Irish and Norsemen. More Round Towers were built in the eleventh and twelfth centuries in order to meet this threat.

A number of these elegant towers have survived in Leinster. Two in County Dublin, at Clondalkin and at Lusk, still have their original conical caps. The conical roof of the Round Tower, which rises to a height of over thirty meters at Glendalough, County Wicklow, has been rebuilt with the original stones. Towers of this height were not rare; one example, which has eight floors, can be seen at Grangefertagh in County Kilkenny, and at Kilree in the same county is another, but it has lost its conical roof, as has the tower, which stands a little to the south of St. Canice's Cathedral in the town of Kilkenny. Other Round Towers of this height have survived at Timahoe, County Leix, where there is a well-preserved one of unusually broad girth with a finely ornamented Romanesque doorway, and at Kells in County Meath where there is the one in which a claimant to the High Kingship was murdered in 1076. In County Kildare there are the stumps of several Round Towers; the one beside Kildare Cathedral had its conical cap replaced by a stepped parapet, one at Taghadoe had no windows at the top and appears never to have been finished, one at Castledermot, said to have been built by the abbot who died in 919, has an upper part rebuilt in the medieval period. The Round Tower to the top of which one can still climb at Monasterboice in County Louth, once housed at least a part of the monastic library, which was burned in it in 1097. The Round Tower at Clonmacnoise, County Offaly, from the topmost floor of which a watcher could see boats coming up the Shannon, is said to have been built by Fergal O'Rourke, who died in 964; it was repaired after being struck by lightning in 1134.

Another smaller tower on the monastic site is actually attached to the little church called Temple Finghin.

Warfare was endemic in Ireland before the arrival of the Vikings and acts of brutality were not unknown, but they were conducted within the framework of an almost ritual code and they lacked the impact of the Viking onslaughts. It is difficult to assess the extent to which the Viking incursions affected Irish life and institutions. In *The Passing of the Old Order,* a paper read at the first International Congress of Celtic Studies in 1959, Professor Binchy held that the Viking raids had a shattering effect, and to them he attributed a profound transformation in Irish society in the tenth century. But whatever disturbance was caused by the Vikings, it is now admitted that their positive contribution to Irish civilization has been greatly underestimated. Some authorities hold that Irish society was nearly stagnant when the Vikings arrived and gave it fresh impetus.

It is true that the most intense period of Viking attacks on Ireland in the ninth century coincided with a decline in both the art and the economy. After the Viking incursions Scandinavian art forms are found in Irish work: Borre style interlace, for example, on a wooden gaming board found at Ballinderry, County Westmeath; the ribbon-like animals of the Jellinge-style; the Ringerike style which became widespread and was used in the decoration of the Shrine of the Crozier of the Abbots of Clonmacnoise; and the refined tendril ornamentation of the Urnes style which found lodgment in the repertoire of Irish scribes and metalworkers.

In view of recent archeological and art-historical evidence it is necessary to abandon, or greatly revise, the old view of the Scandinavians as marauders and murderers who disrupted a supposedly paradisiacal state of Christian virtue and high artistic endeavor. The Norsemen established settlements, were converted to the local religious beliefs, and eventually were absorbed into the community, although, because of their maritime commercial interests, they remained on the coast.

It is clear that in a region like coastal Leinster, with Scandinavian settlements at Dublin, Dundalk, Wicklow, and Wexford, there was considerable intercourse, intermingling, and intermarriage between the Norsemen and the indigenous inhabitants so that a hybrid Hiberno-Norse population emerged. The Norsemen had carried off Irish as slaves; when the Irish defeated the Norsemen at Glen Mama, County Wicklow, in the year 1000, and marched into Dublin, they retaliated. According to the writer of *Cogadh Gaedhel re Gallaibh* (The War of the Gaedhil with the Gaill): "no son of a soldier or of an officer of the Gaedhil (Gaels) deigned to put his hand to a flail, or any other labour on earth; nor did a woman deign to put her hands to the grinding of a quern, or to knead a cake, or to wash her clothes, but had a foreign man or a foreign woman to work for them."

Hiberno-Norse links are apparent in some of the Icelandic sagas. In the *Bishop's Saga,* a Norseman who is credited with knowing the Irish language well uses the word *Malediarik,* which the Icelandic source translated as "Cursed be thou, O King!" It is not difficult to see in this the original Irish *Mallacht duit a rig.* In the *Flóamanna Saga,* the Vikings, on a raid in Ireland, capture two women; one of the women is able to converse with the raiders and explains that she is partly of Norse descent. After defeat in battle at Tara in 980, Olaf Sihtricsson, known as Olaf or Anlaf Cuaran, King of Dublin, made a pilgrimage to Iona and died there. The Irish High King Brian Ború married Olaf's widow, Gormflaith of Leinster, the mother of Sihtric, the next Norse King of Dublin; she also became the mother of Brian's son Donnchadh, King of Munster. King Sihtric in turn married a daughter of Brian, and his own sister married Maelsechnaill II, who succeeded Brian as High King.

In 1013, King Maelmorda of Leinster went to Munster with a gift to Brian Ború of trees from a forest near Edenderry, County Offaly, to make masts for Brian's ships on the Shannon. Maelmorda's sister Queen Gormflaith was also at Kincora and apparently not well disposed to Brian, who had put her aside and taken on two more wives. When Maelmorda came to his sister to ask her to sew a silver button on his tunic, she threw the garment into the fire and declared that he was not worthy to be her brother because of his cowardly subservience to Brian. Thus was achieved an alliance between Leinster and Norse Dublin against Brian. On Good Friday, 1014, at Clontarf, on the north side of Dublin Bay, was fought a great battle: the Irish High King Brian Ború defeated the combined forces of his own stepson and son-in-law, Sihtric the Norse King of Dublin, his brother-in-law the King of Leinster, and Sigurd the Stout, the Norse Earl of Orkney. In its broad outline the description of this battle in the Icelandic *Njal's Saga* tallies with Irish accounts. Brian was killed at Clontarf but the battle was won and Scandinavian power was broken.

However, the Norse monarch of Dublin retained his kingdom and continued to harass his neighbors. In 1018 he captured and blinded his cousin, Brian, King of Leinster, the son of his mother's brother; in 1019 he plundered Kells in County Meath, but was checked in 1020 by the King of Leinster, at Delgany, County Wicklow. However, by 1027 he was ready to attack Meath again. But his submission to the Irish High King assured the integration of the Norse population of Dublin in Irish social and political life.

Fifteen years after the battle of Clontarf, this King of Dublin, Sigtryggr Silki-skegg, or Sihtric Silkenbeard, made a pilgrimage to Rome with Flannagan O'Kelly, King of Bregha, a large plain in County Meath. On his return he founded the Church of the Holy Trinity on the site of the present Christ Church Cathedral. The foundation of another Hiberno-Norse church at Dublin, dedicated to Saint Olaf, may have commemorated Sihtric's father or the death of his son Olaf on his way to Rome in 1034. There were several other churches in Dublin prior to the arrival of the Anglo-Normans. Sihtric died while on a second pilgrimage, leaving no son to succeed him, and his daughter Finen, who was a nun, died in the same year.

The coastal settlements were among the Vikings' enduring legacies to Ireland because they became the country's first towns, and they never lost their importance. Dublin, which was already a flourishing seaport in the tenth century, was the principal of the Viking trading centers. Its trade links with Scandinavia, France, Flanders, Germany, and Spain, first made by the Norsemen, have lasted for centuries. Today Dublin is still Ireland's preeminent port as well as the capital of the Republic; it handles half of the country's total imports and domestic exports. The energetic Norse traders introduced to Ireland a system of weights and measures, and at the end of the tenth century silver pennies of high quality, Ireland's first coinage, were minted in the Norse Kingdom of Dublin. These coins, which mostly bore the name of the King, "Sihtric" or "Sihtric Re Dyflin" and his stylized effigy, were modeled on those of King Aethelred II of England; most of them in existence today come from hoards found in Scandinavia and the Baltic countries.

The Annals refer to the foreigners building a fort at Dublin in 840; Dublin is first recorded as a Norse town in the following year. The pagan Viking cemetery at Kilmainham, Islandbridge, about a mile upstream west of the inhabited nucleus, was in use by around 850. Among the early finds excavated there are brooches and tools—knives, hammers, tongs and sickles, cloth-smoothers, spindle whorls; and weapons, among them a magnificent sword made in Norway and some Frankish swords from the Carolingian world, one of which has a silver-inlaid pommel and a name on the hilt—"Hartolfr"—and another name—"Ulfbehrt"—on the blade. This last name appears on weapons found elsewhere in Europe. Despite the number of Vikings settled in Leinster there are very few other documented burials there; a single grave of the ninth century was found at Navan, County Meath, another under a mound at Donnybrook, near Dublin, and one of the early tenth century at Three-Mile-Water, County Wicklow.

Scandinavian place names like Weis-fjord, now
Wexford, and Cairlinn-fjord (Carlingford, County Louth)
have survived, but because they had no fixed surnames,
practicing instead a patronymic system of nomenclature,
family names of Norse origin are rare, although there must
be a large descent in Leinster from the Hiberno-Norse of
the coastal towns, especially Dublin. Harold has survived
both as a family name and a toponym in Harold's Cross
near Dublin, and another surname of Norse origin, quite
common in Leinster, is Sweetman, deriving from *suatman,*
meaning a dark or swarthy man.

The Viking stronghold at Dublin was built on high
ground above the Liffey, the site of the present Dublin
Castle, and therefore a seat of power for over one thousand
years. Near the present St. Andrew's Church was the
Thingmount, where the freemen met in the public
assembly called the *Thing.* From the pre-urban nucleus
around the stronghold, the Hiberno-Norse town stretched
westwards beyond the present Christ Church Cathedral.
The town grew piecemeal, with residential plots of
irregular shape and size. As early as 989, the Irish High
King Maelsechnaill II, after besieging the town and cutting
off its water supply, imposed a tax of one ounce of gold on
every garth in Dublin, to be paid every Christmas Eve.
High Street formed the axis of the western Hiberno-Norse
unit, joined at an angle by Back Lane, and with straight
lanes running down to Cook Street, a street plan which
survived long after the Middle Ages. The Liffey was much
broader; its tidal waters reached the Hiberno-Norse city
wall, part of which has been exposed by recent excavations
at Wood Quay. Excavations in High Street had already
uncovered an important area of the city and with it many
rich finds. The archeologists found that the houses were
constructed of wattle panels supported by timber posts and
that they had stone-lined hearths in the center of the floor.
Alcoves in the houses were made to contain settle beds.
Fire was a constant hazard, and when a house was
destroyed by fire, a new one was built right on top of it.
The domestic cesspits were found to contain cockle and
mussel shells, indicating that shellfish made up a large part
of the diet of the Hiberno-Norse inhabitants.

The Corporation of Dublin purchased and cleared the
area below Christ Church Cathedral and above Wood
Quay with the intention of building a block for the
Council's offices.

Archeologists, who were allowed to excavate, discovered
extensive remains of the Hiberno-Norse city, including
rows of tenth-century dwellings and domestic objects.
These finds inspired Seamus Heaney's *Viking Dublin: Trial
Pieces*:

I

It could be a jaw-bone
or a rib or a portion cut
from something sturdier;
anyhow, a small outline

was incised, a cage
or trellis to conjure in.
Like a child's tongue
following the toils

of his calligraphy,
like an eel swallowed
in a basket of eels,
the line amazes itself

eluding the hand
that fed it,
a bill in flight,
a swimming nostril.

II

These are trial pieces,
the craft's mystery
improvised on bone:
foliage, bestiaries,

interlacings elaborate
as netted routes
of ancestry and trade.
That have to be

magnified on display
so that the nostril
is a migrant prow
sniffing the Liffey,

swanning it up to the ford,
dissembling itself
in antler combs, bone pins,
coins, weights, scale-pans.

III

Like a long sword
sheathed in its moisting
burial clays,
the keel stuck fast

in the slip of the bank,
its clinker-built hull
spined and plosive
as Dublin.

And now we reach in
for shards of the vertebrae,
the ribs of hurdle,
the mother-wet caches—

and for this trial piece
incised by a child,
a longship, a buoyant
migrant line.

IV

That enters my longhand,
turns cursive, unscarfing
a zoomorphic wake,
a worm of thought

I follow into the mud.
I am Hamlet the Dane,
skull-handler, parablist,
smeller of rot

in the state, infused
with its poisons,
pinioned by ghosts
and affections,

murders and pieties,
coming to consciousness
by jumping in graves,
dithering, blathering.

V

Come fly with me,
come sniff the wind
with the expertise
of the Vikings—

neighbourly, scoretaking
killers, haggers
and hagglers, gombeen-men,
hoarders of grudges and gain.

With a butcher's aplomb
they spread out your lungs
and made you warm wings
for your shoulders.

Old fathers, be with us.
Old cunning assessors
of feuds and of sites
for ambush or town.

VI

"Did you ever hear tell,"
said Jimmy Farrell,
"of the skulls they have
in the city of Dublin?

White skulls and black skulls
and yellow skulls, and some
with full teeth, and some
haven't only but one,"

and compounded history
in the pan of "an old Dane,
maybe, was drowned
in the Flood."

My words lick around
cobbled quays, go hunting
lightly as pampooties
over the skull-capped ground.

When the Council proposed to stop excavation and begin building offices, a group called the Friends of Medieval Dublin led by an Augustinian priest, Francis X. Martin, who is a professor of history at University College, Dublin, challenged the city authorities by asking the judiciary to have the site declared a national monument and applied for an interim injunction to restrain them from going ahead. The preservationists won the day and obtained the definition of part of the Wood Quay site as a National Monument in 1978. When, nevertheless, the city authorities were given permission by the government to send in their bulldozers, there was a public outcry: seventeen thousand men, women and children joined a march from the National Museum to Wood Quay on September 30, 1978 to protest the erection on the site of an office block. Led by the band of the Irish General Transport and Workers Union, followed by the minority of city aldermen in favor of preservation, wearing their black and blue and green robes, the marchers sang the words of the popular old Dublin ballad, *Molly Malone*. Almost the municipal anthem, it is a reminder of the "shambles" of Fishamble Street adjacent to Wood Quay where fishmongers were allowed to dwell in medieval times, and of the mounds of cockle and mussel shells from Hiberno-Norse Dublin, found during the excavations.

The Wood Quay controversy became hot; for months Ireland's most prestigious daily paper, the *Irish Times,* published letters from readers to the editor on the issue. The majority were in favor of preservation, but there were also letters from anticonservationists. A Dublin woman, Eileen Lambert, wrote that an office block on the site in front of "dark old Christ Church" would be much less of an "eyesore" than American tourists "gawking stupidly" at a National Monument; a woman from New York passing through Dublin replied, giving her hair and eye coloring, waist and bust measurements, and enquired whether she was really a greater eyesore than an office block. The redoubtable Eileen returned to the epistolary fray with all the vigor of the Christian Irish women who hooked off one another's heads in battle. "To hell with these nit-wit academics, well-heeled culture-vultures from Foxrock and Dalkey, all these excitable schoolchildren, all these senators out to make a bit of political capital for themselves. The Vikings were an avaricious, brutal, illiterate pack of pagan savages. All they ever did for Ireland was pillage monasteries and split people's heads with axes. Their symbol should be the pig.... For the relics of holy Viking pigs, Dublin is being indefinitely denied its Civic Offices."

Dubliners are more often short of cash than they are of words, as this conversation about the Wood Quay controversy, overheard in a bar, makes clear:

"The decision is a difficult one," observed the publican. "There are many facets to the question."

"Oh you are right there Michael," said the customer, "it is a facetious matter altogether."

"The Lord Mayor is obstreperous and empirical," Michael went on. "He will not be budged and he is not at all concerned if the sight of Christ Church Cathedral is irremediably disimproved."

"Oh you are right there Michael," the customer concluded, "there is no reluctance in him. His obduracy is flagrant."

At a public meeting in the Dublin Mansion House, Professor Kevin B. Nowlan called on the County Council to build their offices on the wastelands which they had created.

Altogether it was the best row Dublin had had for decades, but in the alignment of the conservationist and anticonservationist there was more than a mere interest or disregard for the historic site; there was a basic concern for the exploitation and rape of the city center by speculators and faceless civil servants, and just below the surface a confrontation between the cosmopolitan outlook of Ireland as a multicultural part of Europe, on one side, and the old specter of narrow-minded nationalism on the other.

When the Normans arrived in Leinster they took over the established Hiberno-Norse towns like Dublin, which certainly existed before King Henry I, giving it its first charter in 1172, granted the city to his men of Bristol. On the ridge where the Norse stronghold stood, in compliance with King John's order of 1204, work began on a tower to which a castle and bailey could be added, with a strong curtain wall and ditch. By 1214 the castle was reasonably complete; four towers guarded a walled rectangular enclosure roughly corresponding to the upper yard of the castle as it is today. The Anglo-Normans reclaimed the land between the old wall and the present bank of the Liffey, and on the site of the Hiberno-Norse Holy Trinity they began the erection of Christ Church Cathedral in the 1180s. The design followed experiments in Early Gothic in the West of England, and for the work both materials and masons were imported from England. Anglo-Norman and English clerics were brought over to Ireland to insure a loyal ecclesiastical faction. It was a powerful demonstration to the inhabitants of the sophisticated Anglo-Norman culture.

Among the clerics was Giraldus Cambrensis, so called because he came from Wales where many of the Norman adventurers in Ireland had estates. Gerald's acute observations of Ireland are colored by his attachment to his native Wales and his conviction of the superiority of the Anglo-Normans over the Irish; he also subscribed to the prevailing attitudes of the early medieval clerical world. Gerald's *Topography of Ireland* provides a fascinating picture of late twelfth-century Ireland from the Norman viewpoint:

Ireland is the most temperate of all countries. Snow is seldom, and lasts only for a short time. There is such a plentiful supply of rain, such an ever-present overhanging of clouds and fog, that summer scarcely gives three consecutive days of really fine weather. Winds are moderate and not too strong. The winds from the west-northwest, north and east bring cold. The northwest and west winds are prevalent, and are more frequent and stronger than other winds. They bend (in the opposite direction) almost all the trees in the west that are placed in an elevated position, or uproot them.

Ireland is a country of uneven surface and rather mountainous. The soil is soft and watery, and even at the tops of high and steep mountains there are pools and swamps. The land is sandy rather than rocky. There are many woods and marshes; here and there there are some fine plains but in comparison with the woods they are indeed small. The country enjoys the freshness and mildness of spring almost all the year round. The grass is green in the fields in winter just the same as in summer. Consequently, the meadows are not cut for fodder, and stalls are never built for the beasts.

The land is fruitful and rich in its fertile soil and plentiful harvests. Crops abound in the fields, flocks on the mountains, wild animals in the woods, it is rich in honey and milk. Ireland exports cowhides, sheepskins and furs. Much wine is imported. But the island is richer in pastures than in crops, and in grass rather than grain. The plains are well clothed with grass, and the haggards (farmyards) are bursting with straw. Only the granaries are without their wealth. The crops give great promise in the blade, even more in the straw, but less in the ear. For here the grains of wheat are shrivelled and small, and can scarcely be separated from the chaff by any winnowing fan. What is born and comes forth in the spring and is nourished in the summer and advanced, can scarcely be reaped in the harvest because of the unceasing rain. For this country more than any other suffers from storms of wind and rain.

The invader barons and knights wanted none but the best land that was available, in particular, fertile well-drained plowland, and they soon won great areas of the best agricultural land in the country. Not for them subsistence farming; they looked on land as an investment and were willing to put money into its improvement. They introduced their system of feudal land management and to their manorial estates, spurred on by a population explosion in England, land-hungry farmers came as tenants.

Southeastern Leinster, which the Anglo-Normans discovered first, was particularly inviting. Wexford has a flat coastline because glacial drifts buried almost all the rocks. This corner of Ireland looks a good deal like the West of England and parts of Wales. Even today, with its English-type hedgerows and neat farmhouses with flower gardens, it is not typically Irish. County Wexford is called "The Garden of Ireland" because it has the highest proportion of arable land in the country with 90 percent of its land improved. The Anglo-Normans made it the "Normandy of Ireland," imposing their feudal manorial system. The field-patterns of their settlement have mostly vanished, but in places in Leinster the curving field boundaries which were created by their arcuate plow furrows have survived. Their descendants still bear names imported from England, like Rossiter, concentrated in the Barony of Forth where the first of the name came with the first wave of immigrants after the invasion; Sinnott, Esmond, and Furlong, often thought of now as Irish names; Stafford and Codd, and Wadding, Keating, Devereux, and Hore of Norman origin; and Meyler from Wales. Centuries later, men bearing these names were among the rebels who took part in the Rising of 1798, and particularly in Wexford, massacred later settlers.

Where they found good soil, or where there was a strategic position to be defended, the Anglo-Normans put down roots, and built castles, churches, and manor houses. A typical manorial unit of about 3,000 acres comprised a manor house within a walled bawn, often also moated, and with a motte, or later a tower, for defense. Within the bawn would be other buildings: barns, a byre, a threshing house, and a columbarium. There would also be a water mill on the estate for grinding corn, both for the lord of the manor

and for the tenants, who had to pay for its use. The Irish villeins were recompensed for their labor with the use of a strip of land and access to common pasturage. Goosefoots were usually grown in the strips, while in their broad fields the lord of the manor and the important tenant farmers grew such lucrative crops as wheat, oats, peas, beans, and flax.

For nearly two hundred years, from their arrival in 1170 until the Black Death, which struck in 1350 and decimated the population, the Anglo-Norman oligarchy imposed itself, particularly in Leinster. Remains of their mottes still mark the landscape; there is a tall one, for example, at Granard, in County Longford. There are also substantial remains of their earliest ambitious stone castles, like the rectangular keep with flanking drum towers of Carlow Castle on the route from the central plain of Leinster into Munster, Ferns Castle in County Wexford, first mentioned in a document of 1232, and Kilkenny Castle, heavily rebuilt in the nineteenth century. Sometimes only a donjon or keep was built within a ward and an outer curtain wall, like the ruined tower on the hill of Dunamase in County Leix. Sometimes, as in the case of the royal castle overlooking the Boyne at Trim in County Meath, it was a massive complex; the bailey at Trim, which had two entrances, both protected by barbicans, covered about three acres. These ruins inspired Thomas Kinsella's *King John's Castle*, which begins:

Not an epic, being not loosely architectured,
     But with epic force, setting the head spinning
With the taut flight earthward of its bulk, King John's
     Castle rams fast down the county of Meath.
This in its heavy ruin. New, a brute bright plateau,
     A crowded keep plunging like a bolt at Boyne water,
It held quivering under its heart a whole province of Meath.

Castles were usually built in a prominent position, like the de Verdons' Castleroche on a remote rocky outcrop in County Louth. At Leixlip in County Kildare, the early thirteenth-century cylindrical keep above the Liffey has become a functional part of a later building and is still in domestic use, one of many early keeps and vestiges of keeps in Leinster that are still inhabited. Near this castle was once a famous salmon leap, from which the village got its name in the Scandinavian period.

The Anglo-Norman magnates were also great church-builders. They endowed magnificent new monastic foundations, like the Abbey built between 1204 and 1207 for Cistercians from Stanley in England, on a picturesque loop of the Barrow in the hill-girt Graiguenamanagh basin.

Its cathedral-sized church was modeled on the recently completed church of Stratas Florida Abbey in Wales.

Dunbrody Abbey, County Wexford, was founded in 1180 by Hervé de Montmorency, the uncle of Strongbow and seneschal of his Irish estates, who, after a turbulent secular life, became the first abbot. The ruins impart some of its former grandeur. Dunbrody was a daughter-house of the pre-Anglo-Norman St. Mary's Abbey in Dublin which was, in turn, colonized from Savigny in France. Tintern, also in County Wexford, was another Anglo-Norman Cistercian foundation; its monks came from Tintern in Wales. The Irish Tintern was founded by William, the Earl Marshal, whose wife Isabel was the daughter of Strongbow by his wife Aoife (Eva), the daughter of Dermot, King of Leinster. The Earl Marshal and his wife also founded a parish church of cathedral-like proportions, St. Mary's, at New Ross, which was becoming a thriving port. At Fore, in County Westmeath, the de Lacys built a monastery for the Benedictines, a daughter-house of Evreux in Normandy. The Cistercian Abbey at Baltinglass in County Wicklow had been founded in 1148 by King Dermot of Leinster; under the Anglo-Normans, in the 1180s, three daughter-houses of Baltinglass were established: Monasterevan in County Kildare, Abbeyleix in County Leix, and Jerpoint in County Kilkenny, of which there are magnificent remains. Coal measure sandstone from Castlecomer was used in the building of Jerpoint Abbey, and the local bluish limestone for St. Canice's Cathedral at Kilkenny, the finest large Gothic structure in the country. At Ferns too, a cathedral was built, and in Dublin City, a second cathedral, dedicated to Saint Patrick; it is the largest ancient cathedral in Ireland.

The Crown created a protected area of settlement in northeastern Leinster known as the Pale. Some of the original Irish inhabitants of the province retreated to the bad lands beyond the Pale, like the mountains of Wicklow, or to its eastern marches. The newcomers established themselves wherever there was good land. Their descendants, there today, most of them thoroughly hibernicized, are distinguishable only by their surnames of English, Welsh, or Norman origin—Preston, Plunket, Cusack, and D'Arcy on the fertile grazing lands and prosperous plains of Meath, Dillon also in Meath, and in Westmeath along with Tyrell, Tuite, FitzSimon (Fitzsimmons), and the Petit family, lords of the important market-town of Mullingar; in County Louth, Dowdall, Pipard, which in time became Peppard, Bellew, Taaffe, and Gernon, now generally distorted to Garland; in County Dublin, Bagot, Sarsfield, Luttrell, Delahyde, Talbot, Barnewall, Saint Lawrence, Cruise, Archbold, and Segrave;

in County Kilkenny, Archer, Grace, Forestal, Comerford, Cantwell, Shortall, Rothe, Archdeacon, and branches of the great family of Butler; and in the good lowland pastures of County Kildare, Fitzgerald, Bermingham, Sutton, Aylmer, Wogan, Sherlock, White, and Eustace among others. Later arrivals, like the Lattins, Brabazons, Mastersons, and Bathes, also became prominent in the medieval administration of the Pale. Outside the sphere of Dublin control, the families of Anglo-Norman origin on the marches of the Pale like the Dillons, Daltons, Tyrells, and Delamers in western Meath, which was shired as County Westmeath in 1543, were so Gaelicized that they practiced inheritance and succession, not according to the English system, but by the ancient laws of tanistry and gavelkind. Donagh MacDonagh wrote *A Warning to Conquerors*:

This is the country of the Norman tower,
The graceless keep, the bleak and slitted eye
Where fear drove comfort out; straw on the floor
Was price of conquering security.

They came and won, and then for centuries
Stood to their arms; the face grew bleak and lengthened
In the night vigil, while their foes at ease
Sang of the strangers and the towers they strengthened.

Ragweed and thistle hold the Norman field
And cows the hall where Gaelic never rang
Melodiously to harp or spinning-wheel.
Their songs are spent now with the voice that sang;

And lost their conquest. This soft land quietly
Engulfed them like the Saxon and the Dane—
But kept the jutted brow, the slitted eye;
Only the faces and the names remain.

The Irish, like the O'Byrnes and the O'Tooles in the wilds of County Wicklow, like the MacMurroughs, Kavanaghs, and Kinsellas in northern Wexford and the Blackstairs Mountains, in Counties Leix and Offaly, like the O'Mores and O'Dunnes of Iregan, like the O'Dempseys of Clanmaliere, and like the O'Carrols, O'Molloys, and a branch of the O'Conors, continued to harass the Anglo-Norman settlement. Within the Pale, the most densely settled part of Ireland, the presence of Irish tenantry did not alter the basically English structure of society. Over the centuries the Crown made unsuccessful efforts to preserve the Englishness of this society by such measures as the Statutes of Kilkenny, which outlawed Irish-speaking priests in the Pale, intermarriage between persons of settler descent and the Irish, Irish names, and even Irish dress, games, and such customs as riding bareback.

Eventually the Pale shrank to a smaller area around Dublin, with most of County Meath, parts of County Kildare and the southern part of County Louth. An Act of Parliament was passed in 1494 to have a ditch dug along the frontiers of this shrunken Pale to prevent cattle raids. But the extent of the Pale was further diminished by Irish encroachment, so that by 1537 it did·not even reach as far south as Dalkey in County Dublin. In an effort to hold the territory, the Crown had encouraged the residents of the Pale to build small castles on their estates. The fortified residences, known as tower houses, which were built in the fifteenth and sixteenth centuries, are still a conspicuous feature of the countryside. The three, four or five-story rectangular stone towers, now often creeper-clad, like the fortified churches of Meath, stand as reminders of the precarious tenor of daily life in days gone by.

The walled towns of the Anglo-Normans have been largely rebuilt so that the medieval heritage of a number of Leinster towns is not immediately apparent. The medieval street plan is evident at Kilkenny, where a network of narrow lanes and steps behind the Tholsel on the town's main axis survives. A few late medieval stone houses also survive and there are fragments—windows, gateways, chimney pieces, and armorial slabs. At Carlingford in County Louth, once an important town, are remains of late medieval town tower houses, of which the most interesting is called The Mint. The convoluted street plan of a smaller town in County Louth, Duleek, betrays its medieval origins; so too do the plans of Clondalkin and Lusk in County Dublin, and Trim in County Meath. All but the church of Bannow, a thriving medieval coastal town in County Wexford, now lies buried beneath the majestic dunes, which encroached gradually as the coastal sands shifted. The dunes derived from extensive glacio-fluvial deposits and the fine-grained sediment has also formed the offshore sandbanks on which ships were wrecked. Clonmines, also in County Wexford, was a lead-mining and silver-mining town in the Middle Ages with elegant stone buildings and a busy port. It was transformed into a ghost town by the silting up of its harbor, but several of the principal buildings remain.

Under Edward VI, the Crown built strongholds in Offaly and Leix, Fort Governor and Fort Protector, which became the towns of Philipstown (now Dangan) and Maryborough (now Portlaoise) in the reign of Mary Tudor and her consort Philip of Spain. The confiscated lands became King's County and Queen's County, two-thirds of which were allotted to English settlers. Elizabeth I's determined effort to extend the Crown's authority resulted in the enlargement of the Pale again. At the end of the sixteenth century it embraced most of the present province of Leinster. After a period of national resurgence during which a provisional government with elected representatives was set up at Kilkenny, the seventeenth-century wars further reduced Irish resistance. Cromwell's drastic campaign ended the civil war. He landed in Dublin in August, 1649 and began his grim march through Leinster with an army of ten thousand. At Drogheda he massacred about two thousand officers and men of the town's defeated garrison and indiscriminately slaughtered some priests and other inhabitants. The garrisons of Dundalk and Trim fled when this news reached them. The Cromwellians returned to Dublin and marched south along the coast through Wicklow and Arklow, and then via Ferns and Enniscorthy to Wexford, where, after a successful siege, they killed about two thousand people in another atrocious bloodbath. Faced with this policy of terror, New Ross surrendered without resistance in October. Cromwell bridged the Barrow, crossed County Kilkenny, and in November crossed the Suir into Munster.

After the Restoration, under the aegis of the Viceroy Ormonde, Dublin entered upon an era of building and expansion. From his time dates the creation of the vast royal deer park, now the Phoenix Park, covering 1,752 acres, where deer, cattle, and sheep still graze on the edge of the busy city. The gardens of Saint Stephen's Green in the city are also a result of Restoration urban development, when a former common was turned into a municipally owned square of twenty-seven acres around whose periphery plots were distributed by ballot on leases to gentlemen and citizens of substance. New bridges were built across the Liffey and a fashionable residential area was developed on the north side, around Capel and Mary Streets. The Viceroy was also active in building on his own estates and transformed his ancient castle at Kilkenny into something more like a French château.

It is not the work of the seventeenth century, however, that gave Dublin and many of the towns and villages of Leinster their present aspect and personality, but the ambitious building and development of the eighteenth century. Despite the ravages of poverty, neglect, vandalism, and the speculator's demolition squads, Dublin still has some Georgian elegance, some of it more seedy than smart, but often beautiful in its very shabbiness. Everywhere in Dublin are reminders of its status as the second city of the British Empire, of the glamorous period in which Handel's Messiah was first performed there and Swift was Dean of

Saint Patrick's. Dublin in the nineteenth century was the birthplace of a galaxy of men of letters: James Lever, Joseph Sheridan Le Fanu, Dion Boucicault, Oscar Wilde, George Bernard Shaw, W. B. Yeats, J. M. Synge, Oliver St. John Gogarty, Sean O'Casey, James Joyce, and in the present century, Samuel Beckett.

In the country, landlords who were committed to improvement left an indelible stamp on little towns all over the province. At Celbridge in County Kildare a broad main street leads to the gates of the long tree-lined avenue to Mr. Conolly's Castletown House; Kildrought House, in its own grounds, and rows of neat terrace houses face the street. At the other end of the village are two mansions. Oakly Park was built in 1724 for the Vicar, who was an unsuccessful suitor of his neighbor in Celbridge Abbey. The Vicar was Arthur Price who later, as Archbishop of Cashel, unroofed the medieval cathedral on the Rock; the neighbor he wooed was Esther Vanhomrigh, who more famously played Vanessa to Dean Swift's Cadenus. Swift and Vanessa talked and dallied in the peaceful gardens of the Abbey, where a romantic spot is still remembered as "Vanessa's Bower."

Lord Langford's pleasantly situated little Summerhill in County Meath, planned with not more than fifty houses, Lord De Vesci's Abbeyleix in County Leix, the Duke of Leinster's Maynooth in County Kildare, Lord Wandesford's Castlecomer in County Kilkenny, whose handsome wide main street reflects the former prosperity of the neighboring coalfields, and Lord Farnham's Newtown-Barry, now called Bunclody, on the confluence of the Clody and the Slaney in County Wexford, are all fine examples of gracious eighteenth-century landlord towns and villages. So is the Tynte family's Dunlavin, in County Wicklow, with its delightful colonnaded and domed courthouse. The elegant tree-shaded mall of Georgian terrace houses, which leads from the castle gates to the Protestant parish church at Birr in County Offaly, is an example of an early nineteenth-century improvement; it was planned and laid out for the Earl of Rosse in the 1820s. About the same time the Countess of Belvedere improved Tyrrellspass in County Westmeath. Another successful and attractive early nineteenth-century project was on Lord Fitzwilliam's lands in County Wicklow, the estate village of Shillelagh, named for the celebrated forest of the region, from which, it is believed, timber was sent to England at the end of the eleventh century to roof Westminster Hall. Instead of stucco and whitewash, common to rural Irish dwellings, the houses are built of a mixture of the local granite and schist. The cornerstones, lintels, and jambs are all of granite and inside the houses the stairs are slabs of granite. Among the landlord's improvements made there

by 1840 were a free nondenominational school and a lending library, and adjacent to the village, flour, carding, and bone mills, and a bleaching green. Unfortunately such enlightenment was rare.

The Land Act of 1903, to which compulsory purchase powers were added later, was to change the landscape again since it led to the breakup of many large estates and the proliferation of small owner-occupied farms. The first forestry center, established in 1903, marked the first step in a program of reforestation aimed at restoring Ireland's woodlands, a program which has been expanded and accelerated by the government over the last three decades. In 1946, bog development was nationalized; within twenty-five years of this move four million tons of peat were being cut annually from 135,000 acres of bog. Moss peat, light, fibrous, slightly decayed turf with a great capacity to retain water and air, and virtually useless as fuel, is now being exploited for use in horticulture. Mixed with soil it assists the watering and aeration of flowers and vegetables and promotes their food-retention; it is also useful as a growing medium for mushrooms, tomatoes, and other vegetables. One factory producing moss peat is at Kilberry, County Kildare, where it will take another eighteen years to exhaust the supply of a 2,500-acre bog, after which milled peat will be produced.

Despite changes that have caused concern to environmentalists and ecologists, and despite its long history of settlement, Leinster still offers unspoiled landscapes as well as man-made improvements. In this decade housing estates have mushroomed in those rural areas that are in easy reach of larger towns, encroaching upon the grazing and fattening pastures of Meath and Kildare, and disfiguring the skyline with television aerials. Many of these unsightly developments also lack adequate recreational, educational, and social amenities. Some industrial development too has been detrimental to the environment. A streamless gorge remains, for instance, where the River Liffey was robbed of its waterfall for a hydroelectric scheme which did, however, create the attractive artificial lake of the Poulaphouca Reservoir. Far more melancholy is the denuding of the Leinster Blackwater, an affluent of the Boyne, or the remorseless spoil-heaps and abandoned mine shafts which gash the Vale of Avoca, where copper and iron ores have been exploited since the eighteenth century. Even though three million tons of ore have been taken over the last hundred years, it is estimated that there is still a reserve of twenty-two million tons. The deciduous woodland which clothes the steep hillsides of the valley has been cleared in places to accommodate the industrial waste in this region of natural loveliness made famous by the lines of Thomas Moore's *The Meeting of the Waters*: "There is not in this wide world a valley so sweet/As that vale in whose bosom the bright waters meet." Despite the blight of concrete rectangles, some of the former beauty clings to the place where the Avonbeg and the Avonmore rivers meet. Other places praised by poets have scarcely changed, if at all. F. R. Higgins's "hushed fields of our most lovely Meath" like his loved Boyne in November, "more lake than river, stretched in uneasy light and stript of reeds," still quietly enchant. A verse of Donagh Mac Donagh's *Dublin Made Me* complains of the dullness of the inland plains: "The soft and dreary midlands with their tame canals/Wallow between sea and sea, remote from adventure." But the tame canals have a secretive beauty of their own, less luxurious than the lazy meandering Barrow in its broad valley of lush water meadows, less lovely perhaps than the wooded gorge of the Nore, spanned by the medieval bridge at Inistioge, less idyllic than the Slaney where it flows below the distant granite peaks of the Blackstairs.

Leinster's charm is often intimate; to the casual passerby, the village of Bective in County Meath may seem ordinary enough, but Mary Lavin conveys its private delightfulness in her *Tales from Bective Bridge*: "Do you know Bective? Like a bird in the nest, it presses close to the soft green mound of the riverbank, its handful of houses no more significant by day than the sheep that dot the fields. But at night, when all its little lamps are lit, house by house, it is marked out on this hillside as clearly as the Great Bear is marked out in the Sky. And on a still night it throws its shape in glitter on the water." Among the counties of Leinster, it is Wicklow, however, that takes first place for scenic beauty. The largest area of continuous high ground in Ireland is in Wicklow, with the highest mountain pass roads in the country. One of the great attractions of Dublin is its proximity not only to beaches and harbors, but also to the Wicklow uplands which, although they are only forty minutes away from the city center, have retained a wonderful quality of remoteness, even along the asphalted Military Road which winds through the one-time hideouts for rebels.

J. M. Synge, whose family were landowners in County Wicklow, spent many summers there. Here he wrote of his solitary wanderings that they gave him "a passionate and receptive mood like that of early man." He chose for the action of his dramatic one-act play, *The Shadow of the Glen*, the last cottage at the head of a long glen in County Wicklow. The glen was lonely, wild Glenmalure where the O'Byrnes had defeated the army of Lord Deputy Grey in 1580. Another Wicklow beauty spot, Glenmacnass, with its spectacular waterfall, is remembered in the first verse of Synge's poem, *Queens*:

> Seven dog-days we let pass
> Naming Queens in Glenmacnass
> All the rare and royal names
> Wormy sheepskin yet retains.

Because of its religious associations, Glendalough, once a place of pilgrimage, is the best known of the Wicklow glens. Sir Walter Scott, enchanted by the romantic ruins in their sublime setting, described them as "the inexpressibly singular scene of Irish antiquities." Many visitors see the Cathedral and the quaint little church, called Saint Kevin's Kitchen because of its chimney-like tower, but do not walk as far as the Romanesque ruins of Saint Savior's church where Yeats wrote his *Stream and Sun at Glendalough*.

At the northern end of the Vartry Plateau the white cone of the sharp quartzite peak of the Great Sugar Loaf rises above the gorse and bracken-clad hill slopes. And from these heights there is a wonderful panorama on every side: to the south, the moorlands dotted with little homesteads; to the west, the granite hills of Wicklow pitted with corries and seamed with glacial troughs; to the east, the sea and the coastal marches beyond the woodland gorge of the Glen of the Downs; to the northwest, the Dublin Mountains, which hide the midland plains; to the north, the distant roofs and chimneys and television aerials of Dublin's southern suburbia, and the lovely demesne of Powerscourt with its graceful avenue of slender beeches, and the oak woods of Glencree which inspired Synge's lovely verse in his *To the Oaks of Glencree*.

> My arms around you and I lean
> Against you, while the lark
> Sings over us, and golden lights and green
> Shadows are on your bark.

Synge loved the larks, and regretting his boyhood bird's-nesting he apologized to them and the other birds that nest in the Wicklow Glens in his poem *In Glencullen*:

> Thrush, linnet, stare, and wren,
> Brown lark beside the sun,
> Take thought of kestrel, sparrow-hawk,
> Birdlime and roving gun.
>
> You great-great-grandchildren
> Of birds I've listened to,
> I think I robbed your ancestors
> When I was young as you.

The gardens, Howth Castle, County Dublin. above and below left: *In the spring the rhododendrons are ablaze with color;* right: *The cherry walk in May.*

preceding spread: *This graceful, ancient bridge spans the Slaney at Ballycarney, County Wexford.*

opposite and below: *The gardens at Mount Usher, County Wicklow, were laid out beside a watermill on the Vartry River in the last decades of the nineteenth century by the Walpoles, who own the property to this day. This wonderfully romantic garden, in the style of William Robinson, extends along both sides of the river which forms its principal axis. Only thirty miles from the capital, the garden attracts many visitors.*

The gardens, Mount Usher, County Wicklow.

opposite: *Rich farmland in early autumn, near Dunboyne, County Meath.*

above: *Peat-burning power plant, County Offaly, one of eleven in Ireland.*

below: *Robertstown, County Kildare, a delightful canal village with a handsome eighteenth-century hotel built for the travelers of the once-busy Grand Canal.*

opposite: *A fine example of the Hiberno–Romanesque style, the west doorway of the twelfth-century church, Killeshin, County Leix.*

below: *The tenth-century Glinsk Cross, the garden of Castle Bernard, near Kinnitty, County Offaly.*

opposite: *Shrine to Saint Brigid, near Saint Brigid's Stream, Faughart, County Louth.*

above: *Votive candle in hand, a mother brings her little daughters, as women have done for centuries, to Saint Brigid's Stream. The waters of the spring are credited with miraculous powers. The girls wear their Sunday best for this special outing.*

below: *A Wexford shop window, displaying artificial floral tributes that are placed on graves.*

above: *The capstone of this portal grave, known as the Browneshill Dolmen, in a field near the town of Carlow, is reputed to be the heaviest of any in Europe.*

opposite: *Glendalough, County Wicklow, once a place of pilgrimage, is the best known of the Wicklow glens. Here, Saint Kevin established a community in the sixth century.*

Close to the busy Dublin streets, children enjoy the little park of the handsome King's Inns, begun in 1802.

Dismantled statuary, relics of a bygone imperial age, stored in the courtyard of the late seventeenth-century Royal Hospital, Kilmainham, Dublin.

above: *The arrest of Christ: a detail of one of Ireland's most perfect High Crosses, the tenth-century Cross of Muiredach at Monasterboice, County Louth.*

opposite: *The crossing to the night stairs of the church of the Cistercian abbey at Dunbrody, County Wexford, founded in 1180–1182 by one of the invading Norman knights, who renounced the world and became its first abbot.*

preceding spread: *An elegant ten-arched bridge spans the River Nore at Inistioge in County Kilkenny, one of the most attractive little towns in Leinster.*

above: *The lake of Luggala, County Wicklow, only a few miles from the metropolis.*

opposite: *The tower of the Cistercian abbey at Jerpoint, County Kilkenny, seen through an arch of the fifteenth-century cloister. Founded in the late twelfth century, the abbey was rebuilt in the fifteenth century, when the conspicuous crossing tower was inserted.*

above: *A swan watches over its mate in the park at Castletown House, Celbridge,*
County Kildare. Despite the encroachments of suburbia, the mansion, once the
most sumptuous in Ireland, retains something of its eighteenth-century grandeur.

opposite: *One of the wilder of the Wicklow glens, Glenmalure, the setting for*
J.M. Synge's one-act drama, The Shadow of the Glen.

above left: *This little pink-washed nineteenth-century house at Bannockstown, County Kildare, boasts a glorious cherry tree in its old-world garden.*

below left: *A picturesque estate cottage, Ballymascanlon, County Louth.*

opposite: *Roundwood House, near Mountrath, County Leix, built about 1741 by Anthony Sharp, whose Quaker family had made its fortune in the Dublin wool trade. Acquired by the Irish Georgian Society in 1970, the house has been beautifully restored.*

following spread: *The demesne of Powerscourt, County Wicklow. The beautiful gardens and park were begun in the eighteenth century when the architect Richard Castle built a mansion for Richard Wingfield, M.P., first Viscount Powerscourt.*

above and below: *One of the very few water mills operating in Ireland, Foulkesmill, County Wexford.*

opposite: *Stacking the hay near Kilmore Quay, County Wexford, where smallholders rarely have agricultural machinery. County Wexford is called the Garden of Ireland because it has so much improved land.*

above right: *Courtyard in the Dublin Liberties.*

below right: *Detail of an Italianate building, Essex Quay, Dublin.*

opposite: *Chapel painted in Celtic Revival style by Sister Concepta in Dominican convent, Dun Laoghaire, County Dublin.*

The Four Courts, Dublin.

top right: *A few steps from busy O'Connell Street is Moore Street, where something of an older Dublin survives in the personality of the street traders.*

middle right: *Detail of the Grattan Bridge, Dublin.*

bottom right: *The racecourse at the Curragh, County Kildare, dates from pre-Christian times. The Irish Derby is run here each June.*

MUNSTER

"Lovely the mantle of green"

1	Clonmel	15	Clogher Head	29	River Shannon
2	Ballinatray	16	Cork	30	Limerick
3	River Blackwater	17	Sybil Head	31	Waterford
4	The Burren	18	Cliffs of Moher	32	Helvick Head
5	Bantry	19	Ballinskelligs	33	Kinsale
6	Killarney	20	Doolin	34	Dingle Peninsula
7	Doneraile	21	St. Finan's Bay	35	Tralee
8	Mitchelstown	22	Cashel	36	Ennis
9	Ahenny	23	Dromana House	37	Youghal
10	Staigue Fort	24	Mount Gabriel	38	Adare
11	Nenagh	25	Doonagore Castle	39	The Skelligs
12	Kenmare	26	Kilbarry	40	The Blaskets
13	Ballingarry	27	River Lee		
14	Ballynalackan Castle	28	River Suir		

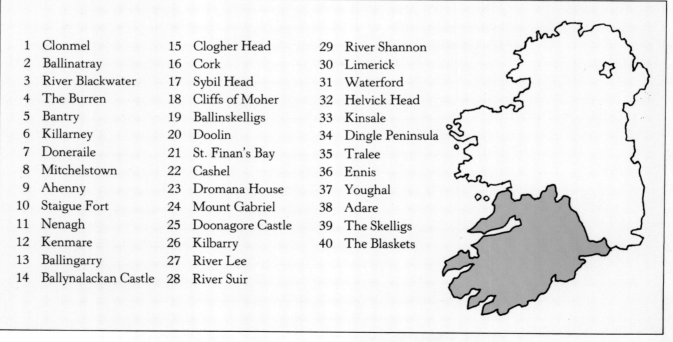

preceding spread: *Doonagore Castle, County Clare, looking out towards the Aran Islands. The circular drum tower on a rectangular plinth, in ruins in the last century, is now a residence.*

When he thought of Connacht, Yeats saw the colors of the Connemara skies, but Munster brought at once to mind the sweet bright green of its lush grasslands and water meadows. And then there are the hundred other shades of green: the menacing green of the foam-capped Atlantic breaking against the Blaskets, the silvery green of the lazy Blackwater as it moves on a sunlit day past Ballinatray to the sea, the green of Gougane Barra lake, sometimes lucent, sometimes obscure and full of mystery. There are the many hues of the patchwork of neat fields and tidy hedgerows of the fertile vales and valleys, the pale fragile green of water lilies in a clotted pond, the sun-dappled green of those delightfully unexpected leafy tunnels formed by the trees arching above the road, the sage green of rushes, the pale delicate green of fern and the rich soft velvety green of moss, the glistening darker green of watercress in a stream, the yet darker green of somber ivy clinging to a ruined tower house, the almost black green of the Irish yews, and the strange blue-green of the mountains which seem to have borrowed blue from the sky.

There are many colors in Munster's palette: the opulent brown of bog freshly cut for turf, the moon-colored sandy strand at Ardmore, the gleaming gray of rain-washed slate, the dazzling whitewash of a farmhouse, or a varicolored streetscape with quaint shopfronts and color-washed houses. Some of nature's colors are bold, like the yellow of the gorse in spring or the strident mauve of the ponticum in bloom; others are bright but exquisite, like the pink and crimson and purple of the riotous hedgerows of fuchsia or the spotted purple and pale mauve of the foxgloves in the hedges. Many others are demure like the springy cushions of silvery-pink sea thrift which cling to the rock face above Ferriter's Cove, muted like the wild thyme on the heaths, or rare and fugitive like the blue patches of spring gentian on the limestone rocks of the Burren in May and the fleeting white flower of the Kerry Lily, a Mediterranean guest who came to Munster and stayed.

Some colors of the province are seasonal: the pearly clusters of bloom on the strawberry trees in the Killarney woods in autumn, the burnished yellow of the haycocks in the fields in late summer, the delicate carpets of white wood anemones in early spring, the muted purple of the blanket of heather over the Knockmealdowns in September. Others are shy, like the dark blue spikes of bugle on the forest edge; some make fragile patterns, like the blackberries in a hawthorn hedgerow or the tufts of Irish saxifrage on the Kerry reeks. And everywhere are the pastures dashed with the creamy pattern of grazing sheep or splashed with the black-and-white and rusty brown coats of the cattle, with here and there a glossy chestnut colt, a satiny black mare or a sleek gray stallion grazing in the shade of beech or sycamore.

Until Tudor times the great valleys of the Blackwater and the Lee were still dense with oak woods. Overall, Munster owes its present character to the changes that began about 1600 when that aspect of Ireland which earned it the name of Emerald Isle started to take shape. The superficial appearance of the landscape was changed by the passes cut through the woods, and then with the extensive woodland clearance for the export of timber. Bridges were built to span the rivers, market towns and nucleated settlements were established where none had been before, and a pattern of arable farming was introduced with small fields enclosed by neat hedgerows. In the eighteenth century more roads were built and farms further improved; the Golden Vale of Tipperary, the Mitchelstown Vale, the luxuriant grasslands of the basins of the Deel and the Maigue rivers, the Vale of Tralee and other flourishing agricultural regions of the province assumed much of their present cultivated appearance. Landlords planned and planted the wooded demesnes which, often having survived the dignified houses which they once graced, are still a pleasing feature of the countryside today.

The history of Munster has been far from peaceful and the prosperity of the fertile vales was until recently enjoyed by few. Even worse poverty and privation prevailed in the bleaker lands to the west, the half-forgotten stony hill country where life is still harsh because the land yields little more to the people than a grasping love which gives scant returns for the passion it arouses and the life's blood it consumes. But much of the land is profoundly tranquil; many of the rivers are still rich with salmon and the lakes with trout; cattle grow fat on the opulent pastures and fair water meadows. For centuries man has responded to Munster's tempting call.

In fact for well over four thousand years vistas of peace and prosperity have attracted man to the southwest of Ireland. Stone Age men reached the region of low hills around Lough Gur in County Limerick where the stone bases of both round and rectangular neolithic dwellings have been discovered. A carbon-14 test on charcoal from a posthole of one of these houses gave a date of about 2530 B.C. The walls of these prehistoric houses would have been constructed of mud and wattle but they were probably roofed with straw. The people of this first settlement cleared the woodland, engaged in simple agriculture, fished in the lake, and hunted. Excavation of seven neolithic residential sites on Knockadoon, a low hill on the lakeside, revealed bones of ox on all seven sites, of pig or boar and also deer on five, of sheep or goat on four, of wolf or dog on three, and of both horse and bear on two.

The Stone Age settlement at Lough Gur prospered. There is evidence of activity there through the Bronze and Iron Ages into the early Middle Ages of our own era. The sod layer is full of shards of prehistoric pottery; many traces of the neolithic inhabitants have survived because the heavy primeval forest was never able to reestablish its growth on the natural limestone terraces and light soil which encouraged the continuity of the settlement. On the townland of Grange, about three hundred meters from the western shore of the lake and close to the present main road from Limerick to Kilmallock, is one of the most impressive stone circles in Ireland, where pagan rituals were performed fifteen hundred to two thousand years before the time of Christ. The date can be deduced from the pottery found inside the circle.

In the hills at Duntryleague in County Limerick, a few miles south of Lough Gur, there is evidence of the passage grave people, who constructed a fine megalithic tomb there with a long entrance passage and a burial chamber built like the passage graves of Brittany.

There is ample evidence of later Stone Age activity in various parts of Munster. In the northwest of the province portal graves were erected in what is now County Clare, of which the best known are the Poulnabrone and Ballyhickey dolmens. In County Waterford at the southeastern extremity of Munster there are also several portal graves; the finest, at Knockeen, was built around 2000 B.C. There are wedge-shaped passage graves in Limerick, Waterford, Clare and Cork counties; at Labbacallee, between Fermoy and Glanworth in County Cork, is the largest one in Ireland, in a cairn bounded by standing stones. Its name in Irish, *Leaba Caillighe,* means "The Hag's Bed" or "The Old Woman's Bed." Perhaps this refers to ancient tales of some great queen of prehistory whose burial place it was reputed to be. When the tomb was excavated in 1934 the bones of a woman were found in the smaller and innermost of the two chambers. There were remains of other inhumation burials in the grave, mostly in the larger chamber, including more human bones, and fragments of a decorated Stone Age pot.

There are several passage graves designated "Diarmuid and Gráinne's Bed." One with this attribution is at Slievenaglasha, County Clare; it is one of several wedge-shaped passage graves in that area. The ancient legend of comely Diarmuid and beautiful Gráinne is similar to that of Tristan and Isolde. Gráinne falls in love with Diarmuid and runs away with him. The lovers are pursued relentlessly throughout Ireland by the jilted warrior Fionn, to whom the wilful Gráinne was betrothed.

In the Bronze Age, the ingenious and industrious metal-prospecting people who reached the shores of Ireland in their search for metal deposits, came as far as the valley of the River Roughty between Kenmare and Kilgarvan in County Kerry. They found metalliferous ores formed from mineral solutions flowing under pressure generated by the intensity of the Armorican earth movements. Copper was the most important of these ores in southwestern Ireland. The Bronze Age metal prospectors also managed to find the copper ores with which the slopes of Mount Gabriel in County Cork are impregnated. Daggers, axes, and halberds were cast from the copper mined there. The same methods of copper mining persisted with barely any change in County Cork for over three thousand years until Cork's Copper Belt was superseded in the last century by the discovery of the copper fields in Rhodesia. These mines remained intact after they were abandoned because blanket bog covered them; they were rediscovered when the bog was cut for fuel. The slopes of Mount Gabriel are a strange lonely place; it is a wondrous and an eerie experience to wander there and ponder on the life of those extraordinary miners and artisans of another age.

The passages into the mine are usually only about 80 centimeters high and one meter, or a little over one meter, wide — just big enough for a man to crawl in and down to the mine, which was usually about 5 meters wide and not more than 1 meter 60 centimeters high.

The stone circles, relics of pagan cult practices, were erected during the Bronze Age and the subsequent Iron Age. The impressive circle already mentioned at Lough Gur is an early example. The circle on a hillside at Drombeg in County Cork was erected later, apparently about the time of Christ. Tests on remains there gave a date between the second century B.C. and the second century A.D., and two round stone huts about 55 meters from the circle can be dated from between the beginning of the second century A.D. and the middle of the fourth. Under a stone in the center of the stone circle the cremated and pulverized remains of a human adolescent were found in a broken pot. The custom of single burial had spread rapidly and widely in the Bronze Age, but the place of the urn in the center of the circle here does suggest that it was connected with cult worship.

There are about fifty known hill forts in Ireland. One of the largest is in Munster, at Moghane in County Clare; it has three concentric banks and ditches. Not far from Moghane, a laborer employed in the construction of the West Clare railway in 1854 stumbled on an enormous cache of late Bronze Age gold objects. Unfortunately most of this priceless hoard was dispersed and lost; the wonderful ornaments were sold for their mere bullion value and probably melted down. However, some of the marvelous pieces from the Great Clare Gold Find did reach the National Museum. That sensational find was the largest of prehistoric gold, but there were other important finds and surely there must still be gold artifacts hidden under the soil of Munster. A number of pieces, mostly votive objects, were found on the Limerick-Tipperary borders in the Bog of Cullen, which consequently earned the name of the Golden Bog.

One splendid example of Bronze Age jewelry found in Munster is the Gleninsheen gorget, named for the place where it was discovered in County Clare. It is a chiseled gold ornament made to be worn under the chin and secured at the shoulders with discs. How magnificent a Munster potentate of the late Bronze Age or the Iron Age must have looked wearing such regalia.

The homesteads of the magnates in the Iron Age would have been the ring forts, which look so much like military fortifications but were in fact defensible residential compounds. There are thousands of these ring forts in the country, many in Munster, and some hundreds alone in the Burren in County Clare. Many ring forts were earthworks, but a number were built with stone walls, of which one of the largest and finest is in western Munster, at Staigue in County Kerry. The circular stone wall, five and a half meters in height and four meters thick, surrounds an area about twenty-eight meters in diameter, where there would have been dwellings. A bank and a ditch surround the whole enclosure. Precious objects of the Early Christian era have been found in some ring forts which remained in residential use for centuries. It is known, for instance, that the circular stone ring fort called Cahermacnaghten, in County Clare, to which a two-storied gateway was added in medieval times, was used in the Middle Ages as a law school by the O'Davoren family, hereditary brehons under the Gaelic social system. The O'Davorens appear to have been still in occupation in the latter part of the seventeenth century when the fort was called "O'Davoren's town" and there was a sizable house inside the enclosure. At Cahercommaun in County Clare, a silver brooch of the ninth century was found in a souterrain of the stone fort built on a cliff edge, but a far more impressive find was the discovery of the famous Ardagh Chalice, an object of the Early Christian church in Ireland which Dr. Kathleen Hughes described as "a triumph of virtuosity and beauty"; it was found in a ring fort at Ardagh in County Limerick.

Saint Patrick, swooping down from the north with a retinue of young noblemen, stopped at the seats of the monarchs to win them, and with them their people, to the new faith. His success at the center of power of the Eoghanachta, kings of Munster, was one of Patrick's important missionary achievements. The royal seat was on a great rock, now called Cashel, which rises dramatically above the plain. Such were Patrick's powers of persuasion, that his biographer records a wonderful incident at Cashel when the saint was baptizing Aenghus, a royal convert. Patrick unwittingly planted his crozier on the prince's foot, spearing it with the spike. The doughty neophyte did not even murmur, supposing the painful wound to be a part of the baptismal ceremony, an initiation into the way of the Cross. As Patrick would surely have preached a graphic account of Christ's crucifixion and agony, Aenghus may have concluded that to follow this Lord he too must be pierced through the foot.

Christianity spread through Munster rapidly, swiftly extending its influence to the extremities of the province, but the ease with which it appears to have embraced the ancient social system was only apparent. Because many of the traditions and the lore of the pagan world were tolerated and not eradicated, a society emerged in which the dominion of the natural, the ancient creed which glorified the instinct, marched alongside the new faith which stressed restraint and preached the doctrine of salvation through repentance and penitence. The persistence of the pagan culture resulted in a veiled but inexorable struggle which lasted for centuries. It could be argued that the complete victory of Christianity was only achieved in the nineteenth century, to flourish fiercely for a hundred years before it was assailed in our time by the new paganism of a modern consumer society.

The duality of the personality affected by the emphasis on carnal pleasure of the pagan culture, and the promise of salvation of the Christian faith, is poignantly expressed in the lament of an Irish woman poet of the ninth century, *The Hag of Beare*, beautifully translated by John Montague:

> Ebb tide has come for me;
> My life drifts downwards
> Like a retreating sea
> With no tidal turn.

I am the Hag of Beare,
Fine petticoats I used to wear,
Today, gaunt with poverty,
I hunt for rags to cover me.

Girls nowadays
Dream only of money—
When we were young
We cared more for our men.

Riding over their lands
We remember how, like nobles,
They treated us well;
Courted, but didn't tell.

Today every upstart
Is a master of graft;
Skinflint, yet sure to boast
Of being a lavish host.

But I bless my King who gave—
Balanced briefly on time's wave—
Largesse of speedy chariots
And champion thoroughbreds.

These arms, now bony, thin
And useless to younger men,
Once caressed with skill
The limbs of princes!

Sadly my body seeks to join
Them soon in their dark home—
When God wishes to claim it,
He can have back his deposit.

No more gamy teasing
For me, no wedding feast:
Scant grey hair is best
Shadowed by a veil.

Why should I care?
Many's the bright scarf
Adorned my hair in the days
When I drank with the gentry.

So God be praised
That I mis-spent my days!
Whether the plunge be bold
Or timid, the blood runs cold.

After spring and autumn
Come age's frost and body's chill:
Even in bright sunlight
I carry my shawl.

Lovely the mantle of green
Our Lord spreads on the hillside!
Every spring the divine craftsman
Plumps its worn fleece.

But my cloak is mottled with age—
No, I'm beginning to dote—
It's only grey hair straggling
Over my skin like a lichened oak.

And my right eye has been taken away
As down-payment on heaven's estate;
Likewise the ray in the left
That I may grope to heaven's gate.

No storm has overthrown
The royal standing stone.
Every year the fertile plain
Bears its crop of yellow grain.

But I, who feasted royally
By candlelight, now pray
In this darkened oratory.
Instead of heady mead

And wine, high on the bench
With kings, I sup whey
In a nest of hags:
God pity me!

Yet may this cup of whey
O! Lord, serve as my ale-feast—
Fathoming its bitterness
I'll learn that you know best.

Alas, I cannot
Again sail youth's sea;
The days of my beauty
Are departed, and desire spent.

I hear the fierce cry of the wave
Whipped by the wintry wind.
No one will visit me today
Neither nobleman nor slave.

I hear their phantom oars
As ceaselessly they row
And row to the chill ford,
Or fall asleep by its side.

Flood tide
And the ebb dwindling on the sand!
What the flood rides ashore
The ebb snatches from your hand.

Flood tide
And the sucking ebb to follow!
Both I have come to know
Pouring down my body.

Flood tide
Has not yet rifled my pantry
But a chill hand has been laid
On many who in darkness visited me.

Well might the Son of Mary
Take their place under my roof-tree
For if I lack other hospitality
I never say "No" to anybody—

Man being of all
Creatures the most miserable—
His flooding pride always seen
But never his tidal turn.

Happy the island in mid-ocean
Washed by the returning flood
But my ageing blood
Slows to final ebb.

I have hardly a dwelling
Today, upon this earth.
Where once was life's flood
All is ebb.

But another woman, Líadan, from Dingle in western Kerry, an accomplished poet and a member of the poet's guild, which necessitated years of study, lamented not her bygone pleasures, but the pain of her rejection of the poet Curithir, whom she loved but refused because of her belief in Paradise. Her pain is expressed in these words, again in John Montague's sensitive translation:

Joyless
what I have done;
to torment my darling one.

But for fear
of the Lord of Heaven
he would lie with me here.

Not vain,
it seemed, our choice,
to seek Paradise through pain.

So our vision of Early Christian society is a complex one, aristocratic and heroic in structure, but a patchwork of austerity and rigid asceticism, mysticism and miracles, high artistic achievement, the power of arms, carnal pleasure and lust. Side by side with the erotic reminiscence of *The Hag of Beare* is this song of the monastic hermit Marban, translated by Michael Hartnett:

For I inhabit a wood
unknown but to my God
my house of hazel and ash
as an old hut in a rath.

And my house small, not too small,
is always accessible:
women disguised as blackbirds
talk their words from its gable.

The stags erupt from rivers,
brown mountains tell the distance:
I am glad as poor as this
even in men's absence.

Death-green of yew,
huge green of oak sanctify,
and apples grow
close by new nuts:
water hides.

Young of all things,
bring faith to me,
guard my door:
the rough, unloved
wild dogs, tall deer,
quiet does.

In small tame bands
the badgers are,
grey outside:
and foxes dance
before my door
all the night.

All at evening
the day's first meal
since dawn's bread:
trapped trout, sweet sloes
and honey, haws,
beer and herbs.

Moans, movements of
silver-breasted birds rouse me:
pigeons perhaps.
And a thrush sings
constantly.

Black-winged beetles
boom, and small bees:
November
through the lone geese
a wild winter
music stirs.

Come fine white gulls
all sea-singing,
and less sad,
lost in heather,
the grouse's song,
little sad.

For music I
have pines, my tall
　　　music-pines
so who can I
envy here, my
gentle Christ?

James Simmons has translated the song of another hermit who has known and renounced bodily pleasure. It begins:

My heart stirs quietly now to think
of a small hut that no one visits
in which I will travel to death in silence.

Nothing will draw my eyes away,
there, from repentance for evil done,
or hinder my view of Heaven and Earth.

In the ninth-century *Instructions of King Cormac*, the questioner asks the king: "What is the sweetest thing you have heard?" and the monarch answers:

Not hard to tell,
the shout of triumph after victory,
praise after wages,
a lady's invitation to her pillow.

In their monastic enclosures the pious monks with equal industry and seriousness copied out the holy gospels and the penitentials of the church and recorded the sagas and myths of the pagan world replete with accounts of lascivious deeds, like the *Leabhar Gabhála* (the Book of Invasions), an account of three men and fifty-one women who indulged in a sexual marathon until the orgy ended with the death of two of the men, spent with passion, and

the disappearance of the third, who fled, "Lest he too, by love be rent."

With the conversion of the ruling house to Christianity, Cashel became, as well as the center of secular power, the seat of ecclesiastical authority, second only in Ireland to Armagh. The present ruined cathedral, which replaced one founded in 1169 by King Domhnall Mor of the O'Brien dynasty, dates only from the thirteenth century. The earliest building of the cluster on the Rock is a small but beautiful church consecrated in 1134. It is called Cormac's Chapel after its founder King Cormac Mac Carthy, a descendant of the old Eoghanachta, who built it in fulfillment of a vow made to Saint Malachy at Lismore. There is certainly no room in Cormac's Chapel for a choir or for many priests at the altar, still less for a "thick line" of people. To judge by the surviving early Christian churches, all diminutive, the church of the earlier Cormac, King-Bishop of Cashel, would have been small too, although admittedly there exists an account of Saint Brigid's monastic church at Kildare in the seventh century which describes it as lofty, spacious and grandly decorated. The surviving early Christian churches in Munster are all of very modest size. There are examples at three places in County Limerick: Kilrush, now engulfed by the suburbs of Limerick City, Killulta, and Mungret. There are more in Western Kerry, whose remoteness appealed to the ascetically inclined Irish monks. Single-cell stone churches can be seen on the Dingle peninsula, where one is constructed like an upturned boat, on one of the Blasket Islands, on Church Island, on one of the Maharee Islands, and on the island of Skellig Michael, lonely Atlantic outposts which were the most westerly inhabited places in Europe. These were all very simple buildings in keeping with the aspirations expressed by Saint Columcille:

On some island I long to be,
a rocky promontory, looking on
the coiling surface of the sea.

To see the waves, crest on crest
of the great shining ocean, composing
a hymn to the creator, without rest.

To see without sadness the strand
lined with bright shells, and birds
lamenting overhead, a lonely sound.

To hear the whisper of small waves
against the rocks, that endless sea-
sound, like keening over graves.

To watch the sea-birds sailing
in flocks, and most marvellous
of monsters, the turning whale.

(Version: John Montague)

In Ireland, the Romanesque style was tailored to suit the local needs and the small church buildings which were the norm. In the process of adaptation indigenous traits were assimilated, so that the Hiberno-Romanesque style peculiar to Ireland evolved its own repertoire which included, with the established motifs, vernacular elements and art forms brought from Scandinavia to Ireland by the Vikings. The Norsemen had founded two of the three cities of Munster in the ninth century: Waterford—where they consolidated their power with the arrival of a great fleet in 914—and Limerick, and by their mercantile settlement promoted the development of the third city, Cork, originally a monastic foundation of Saint Finnbarr. In all three cities they set up little independent kingdoms. Two prominent County Limerick surnames, Arthur and Harold, hark back to Viking times; Trant, commonest in Kerry, is also of Norse origin.

The early churches of Lismore, County Waterford, a renowned center of spirituality and learning in Munster, have vanished, but excellent examples of Hiberno-Romanesque work have survived in the province. At Toureen Peekaun in County Tipperary there is an out-of-the-way, simple little ruined church with a window which has the Romanesque chevron decoration; the ruined church of Saint Farranan at Donaghmore in the same county is a nave-and-chancel building which had a fine Romanesque west doorway, now unfortunately marred by damage. Only the elegant five-bay facade survives of the Romanesque church of Saint Cronan at Roscrea, County Tipperary. The ruined church at Monaincha, also in County Tipperary, has a Romanesque west doorway and chancel arch. According to the twelfth-century chronicler Giraldus Cambrensis, no human female, or even female animal, could enter the monastery at Monaincha; if one did she was sure to die. There are Romanesque church remains in County Kerry, at Aghadoe, built in 1158, at Ardfert, and at Kilmalkedar on the Dingle peninsula.

King Domhnall Mor O'Brien, who was renowned as a church builder, founded the cathedral at Limerick, where parts of the west door date from his time, and the cathedral at Killaloe, County Clare, where the Romanesque doorway of an earlier church on the site has been inserted in the south wall. Beside the cathedral is a small twelfth-century

church, dedicated to Saint Flannan, with a steeply pitched roof and fine Romanesque doorway. Another excellently carved Romanesque door survives in the ruined church at Clonkeen, County Limerick.

Those kings of the O'Brien dynasty belonged to the Dál Cais or Dalcassian sept which had provided the line of rulers in Thomond who had supplanted the supremacy of the Eoghanachta in Munster. Little remains to be seen of their inaugural place, Magh Adhair, near Quin in County Clare, save a high flat-topped mound and a standing stone. It was there, in 877, that Flann, High King of Ireland, sat nonchalantly after defeating King Lorcan of Thomond in battle. To demonstrate the security of his superiority Flann disdainfully began a game of chess. There too, the most famous of the O'Brien kings, BrianBorú, who died in 1014, was inaugurated as monarch. In 977 Brian was crowned King of Munster on the Rock of Cashel; within his Munster dominions the Mac Carthys and O'Sullivans still ruled virtually independent lordships in the southwest.

The O'Briens retained their court at Kincora in County Clare after establishing their ascendancy in Munster. Cashel, which had continued to function as an ecclesiastical capital, was made over to the Church as a gift by King Muirchertach O'Brien in 1101. Henceforth Cashel flourished as an ecclesiastical seat only, and in 1152 became, officially, the head of one of the country's ecclesiastical provinces. The bard of the O'Briens who had known Kincora in its heyday under BrianBorú composed a lament for him and for Kincora's former glory. This romantic translation of two of the verses is by the nineteenth-century poet, James Clarence Mangan:

Oh, where Kincora! is Brian the Great?
And where is the beauty that once was thine?
Oh, where are the princes and nobles that sate
At the feast in thy halls, and drank the red wine?
    Where, oh, Kincora?

Oh, where, Kincora! are thy valorous lords?
Oh, whither, thou Hospitable! are they gone?
Oh, where are the Dalcassians of the Golden Swords?
And where are the warriors Brian led on?
    Where, oh, Kincora?

Today, the question can also be asked: "Where indeed was Kincora itself?" The northern O'Neills wrecked it on a foray into the kingdom of Munster in retaliation for which King Muirchertach O'Brien marched north in 1101 and dismantled their fort, the Grianan of Aileach. Now, the exact site of Kincora is uncertain. It may have been Béal Ború, a large ring fort of the Dál Cais about one mile from Killaloe in County Clare. According to a local tradition Kincora was on the hill in the town itself where the Roman Catholic church now stands.

In Lough Derg, the largest and lowest of the lakes formed by the River Shannon, is Inishcaltra, the Holy Island, where Brian Ború rebuilt the early monastic establishment after it had been plundered by the Vikings on one of their raids up the Shannon, and one of Brian's brothers became the abbot. The ruins of several churches have survived on the little island, of which the most impressive is the one dedicated to the founder of the monastery, Saint Caimin. It has an elegant Romanesque chancel arch and doorway. The Irish have long-lasting attachments to certain burial places and one of these, Holy Island, became a favorite place of penance and pilgrimage, despite the inconvenience of rowing a corpse across the lake, especially in bad weather. But, with its view of the Arra Mountains and the illustrious company of royalty and saints, there can be few more delightful cemeteries in which to awake on the morning of the Resurrection.

Robert FitzStephen, one of the first Norman knights to land in Ireland in 1169, thrust inland as far as Limerick, but he was forced by the Irish to retreat to Leinster. In May, 1170, Raymond FitzGerald, known as Raymond Le Gros, landed at Dundonnell and defeated the men of Waterford; his force was joined by two hundred knights and one thousand troops under a Norman baron from Wales, Richard FitzGilbert de Clare, better known as Strongbow, who landed at Crook in August of the same year. This Norman expedition took Waterford, but then turned north. In October of 1171, King Henry II, who was concerned that Strongbow might carve out for himself a kingdom in Ireland, came over with a fleet of four hundred ships and disembarked four thousand men at Crook. Henry secured the verbal submission of the Mac Carthy chief in the southwest, and of the O'Briens, and a council of bishops swore fealty to him at Cashel. Then, by the Treaty of Windsor in 1175, Henry was recognized by the Irish High King as Lord of Ireland. He parceled out much of Munster to his knights, granting Desmond to Robert FitzStephen and Milo de Cogan, and Thomond to Philip de Braose; the cities of Cork and Limerick were retained by the Crown. De Braose was not able to implement his grant, but Milo de Cogan and Robert FitzStephen established their authority over a considerable area in the south of Munster. The Irish continued a guerrilla warfare from the woods and marshes,

but they were unequal to the sophisticated military tactics of the invaders, who constructed forts to hold their lines as they advanced with their skilled Flemish infantrymen and Welsh archers. The settlement of some of these troops in Ireland accounts for the surnames Fleming and Walsh. The major castles built by the Normans as they advanced into Munster were at Roscrea, Nenagh, and Carrick-on-Suir, all in County Tipperary.

King John granted land in Munster to Theobald Walter, the founder of the Butler family in Ireland, and to William de Burgos, who came over with him in 1180. Theobald set up the lordship of Ormond, and William de Burgos took over a territory in southern Tipperary. By 1200, the FitzGeralds, who had received grants farther west in Limerick and Kerry, had succeeded in pushing the old Irish chiefs back to the southwest. The King, whose policy was to dilute the power of his vassals, finally granted Thomond, where his knights had not managed to establish themselves, to the O'Briens, whose territory it already was.

As they extended their power, the Normans set up towns around their castles. Ten Munster towns are Norman foundations, six in County Tipperary—Roscrea, Nenagh, Carrick-on-Suir, Thurles, Clonmel, and Tipperary; one in County Waterford—Dungarvan; one in County Kerry—Tralee; and two in County Cork—Youghal and Kinsale. The old Viking walled cities of Limerick, Waterford, and Cork continued to flourish as trading ports, and continental trade developed also from Youghal, Dungarvan, and Kinsale. Each port developed special commercial connections with foreign cities: Cork traded mainly with Flanders, Western France, and Spain; Youghal with Lucca and Florence in Italy, as well as with Normandy and Portugal; Waterford, the preeminent port because of its excellent harbor, traded with France, Portugal, and Spain; and Limerick, particularly with the French Atlantic ports of Bordeaux and Bayonne. Wine was the major import, followed by spice, corn, cloth, salt, coal, silk, oil, and raisins. The Irish exported hides, wool, grain, fish, and timber, and later in the Middle Ages, linen and serge. By the thirteenth century the enterprising Italian banking family of Frescobaldi had established branches in Munster, Waterford, Cork, and Youghal, and there were also agents of the Ricardi family of moneylenders. The surname Lombard, still found in County Cork, originally designated a man from Lombardy, but subsequently came to be used generically for a banker.

The towns in Munster achieved a high degree of independence, for in practice they were controlled by a few families who clung tenaciously to their power. In the fourteenth century, as a result of attempts to limit the number of Irish inhabitants and their activities in the towns, Irish communities grew up outside the town walls.

The descendants of the Norman grantees, theoretically subject to royal writ, eventually became virtually independent. Established as feudal lords they held feudal courts and their writ rather than the king's was observed in their territories. This was especially true in the Desmond palatinate, where a great liberty was built up by the FitzGeralds over much of southern and western Munster. A branch of the FitzGerald family which took the patronymic Fitzmaurice established itself in County Kerry. The Butlers in Ormond, who remained the most devoted to the English Crown of the Anglo-Norman families, and the Burkes continued to hold sway in what is now County Tipperary. Most of the families of Anglo-Norman origin became hibernicized, adopting the Irish language and many of the customs, and intermarrying with the Irish. Their descendants, distinguishable from the families of ancient Irish origin only by their surnames, can still be found in the localities where their ancestors settled. There are Aylwards, Wyses, Walls (originally de Valle), and Powers (deriving from le Poer) in County Waterford; Everards, St. Johns, Purcells, and Graces (deriving from le Gras) in County Tipperary; Roches, Barrys, Cogans or de Cogans, and Nagles (deriving from de Angulo) in County Cork; Fitzgibbons, de Lacys, and Walls in County Limerick; Stacpooles in County Clare; and Cantillons (deriving from de Cantelupe) in County Kerry, as well as families with Anglo-Saxon names who have been in Munster since the beginning of the Norman settlement, like the Sarsfields in County Limerick, the Waddings in County Waterford, the Stacks and Ferriters in County Kerry, and the Goulds and Verlings in County Cork.

Throughout the Middle Ages some of the old Irish ruling families, the O'Briens, MacMahons, and Mac Namaras in County Clare, and the Mac Carthys, O'Driscolls, O'Donoghues, and O'Sullivans, who had been pushed back into western Cork and southwestern Kerry, managed to retain some of their authority in an uneasy truce with the distant authorities. Despite population movement and massive emigration, those family surnames are still common in the region.

When the Tudor monarchs embarked on a campaign to extend the royal writ and anglicize the country, they found that they had to combat not only the old Irish, but also contend with the stiff opposition of many of the Hiberno-Norman magnates. The FitzGeralds, Earls of Desmond, were particularly recalcitrant. They had been governing their palatinate in Munster practically as an independent state since Thomas, Earl of Desmond, was executed in 1468 for his dealings with the Irish in defiance of the racial laws. England's break with Rome exacerbated old grievances, and in the reign of Elizabeth I, the Desmond faction, which had remained loyal to the old faith, rose in open rebellion against the Crown and engineered the landing in Munster in 1580 of a Papal expeditionary force of between six and seven hundred men. The invaders, Spaniards and Italians, got no farther than Smerwick Bay in County Kerry where they had landed. They were besieged by the English, forced to surrender, and then all butchered. When the Earl of Desmond was killed in 1583 the power of the family was broken. The Desmond territory, over half a million acres in counties Cork, Limerick, Kerry, and Waterford, was confiscated; the foundation of a new English Munster was laid.

Among the English who received grants of land in the plantation scheme to colonize the forfeited Desmond palatinate were two adventurers who had taken part in the genocide at Smerwick, Sir Walter Raleigh and Edmund Spenser. Raleigh received 40,000 acres, but most of the land was parceled out to the English in estates of 12,000, 8,000, 6,000 and 4,000 acres, to which they brought land-hungry settlers from England. The plantation is often considered a failure, or at best a qualified success, because the settlers were continually harassed by the dispossessed Irish, and some of them, discouraged, returned home. But the fact is that many of the Elizabethan settlers persisted, and their descendants may still be found in Munster today. Quite a number of families of settler descent erroneously dubbed "Cromwellians" have actually been in Cork and Kerry and Limerick since the sixteenth century. The Jephson family at Mallow Castle in County Cork descend from Sir Thomas Norreys, the English Lord President of Munster who was granted the estate in 1584 and whose heiress daughter married Sir John Jephson. The herd of white-grained deer on the Mallow demesne is claimed to have been a gift of Queen Elizabeth I to her goddaughter Elizabeth Norreys. In the same county are the families of Daunt, originally from Gloucestershire, Boyle, Becher, Beamish, Graves, and Gillman, all descended in the male line from Elizabethan settlers, as are the Blennerhassets from Cumberland, Springs from Suffolk, Rices from Wales, and Herberts from the Welsh marches, all settled in County Kerry, and the Bloods from Derbyshire, who came to County Clare.

The poet Edmund Spenser was one of the settlers who did not stay. He was awarded an estate of three thousand acres in County Cork, along with Kilcolman Castle (a former Desmond tower house), and he took up residence there in 1578. While running his new estate he wrote stanzas of *The Faerie Queene*, and his *Veue of the present state of Ireland*, in which he recommended the most extreme measures for the Irish whom he regarded as not much better than animals. He was very suspicious of Waterford and Cork, "those two cytties above all the reste doe offer an ingate to the Spanyarde most fytlie and also inhabytants of them are most ill affected to the Englishe government and moste frendes to the Spanyardes..." His plans for dealing with the Irish included the recommendation that all "'O's and Macs be utterly forbiden and extinguyshed." He was later to recommend not only extinguishing the names but also the people who bore them. Much as he disliked the inhabitants, Spenser was enchanted with the landscape:

All those faire forrests about Arlo hid,
And all that Mountaine, which doth over-looke
The richest champain that may else be rid;
And the faire Shure in which are thousand Salmons bred.

In 1594 Spenser was married in Cork to his second wife, Elizabeth Boyle, the kinswoman of another Elizabethan adventurer Richard Boyle, an energetic colonizer who became Earl of Cork. The poet brought his bride to Kilcolman, and to celebrate his nuptials wrote *Epithalamion*, in some verses of which he extolled the natural beauty of his adopted home:

Ye Nymphes of Mulla which with careful heed,
The silver scaly trouts doe tend full well,
And greedy pikes which use therein to feed,
(Those trouts and pikes all others doo excell)
And ye likewise which keepe the rushy lake,
Where none doo fishes take,
Bynd up the locks the which hang scatterd light,
And in his waters which your mirror make,
Behold your faces as the christall bright...

The "Mulla" of *Epithalamion* is the River Awbeg which watered Spenser's Cork estate. However, the poet's disdain for his dispossessed and impoverished Irish neighbors, and his advocation of the harshest measures of repression, won him no love among them. In 1598 they burned Kilcolman Castle and laid waste the lands. Spenser and his family fled to London. It is believed that one of the Spenser children

and part of the manuscript of *The Faerie Queene* perished in the flames at Kilcolman, but there is no documentary evidence of this. Spenser's son subsequently sold the estate in 1630 to Sir William St. Leger, whose descendants remained there until the present decade when the American heir was unable to prove the legitimacy of his lineage, and Doneraile Court, the mansion built on the lands, was abandoned. The demesne, in which there is a herd of red deer, is to be maintained as a wildlife park.

A twentieth-century writer, Elizabeth Bowen, whose home was near Kilcolman, described the region in her book *Bowen's Court*:

This limestone country is pitted with kilns and quarries; the hard white bye-roads run over rock. Our two rivers, the Funcheon and the Awbeg, have hollowed out for themselves, on their courses south to the Blackwater, rocky twisting valleys. Here and there down the valleys the limestone makes cliffs or amphitheatres. In places the rivers flow between steep woods; in places their valleys are open, shallow and lush—there are marshy reaches trodden by cattle, fluttered over by poplars from the embanked lanes. Herons cross these in their leisurely flopping flight; water peppermint grows among the rushes; the orchis and yellow wild iris flower here at the beginning of June. Lonely stone bridges are come on round turns of the stream, and old keeps or watch towers, called castles, command the valleys: some are so broken and weathered that they look like rocks, some have been almost blotted out by the ivy; some are intact shells whose stairs you can still climb.

There are mills on both rivers—one great mill is in ruins— and swans on the Funcheon and the Awbeg. Not far from the Awbeg, under Spenser's castle, there is a marsh where seagulls breed in spring.

The country is not as empty as it appears. Roads and boreens between high hedges, sunk rivers, farms deep in squares of sheltering trees all combine by their disappearance to trick the eye. Only mountainy farmhouses, gleaming white on their fields reclaimed from the bog, and facades of chapels on hills or hillocks, show. The country conceals its pattern of life, which can only wholly be seen from an aeroplane. This is really country to fly over—its apparent empty smoothness is full of dips and creases. From the air you discover unknown reaches of river, chapels, schools, bridges, forlorn graveyards, interknit by a complex of untravelled roads.

And of the Doneraile demesne she wrote:

Lying along the Awbeg, with its rocks and willows, the demesne of Doneraile is a lyrical place. Carriage drives loop about; there are bamboo groves, a soporific lime walk, a clotted lily pond. The demesne was dear to several Elizabethans— Raleigh, Spenser and Sydney all conversed here, strolling along the lime walk or reclining among "the cooly shade of the green alders," Edmund Spenser recalls.

The general insurrection of the native Irish, which began in Ulster in the autumn of 1641, spread rapidly through the country, and in 1642 the people of Munster rose and attacked the settlers. During the Civil War the eastern part of the province was again the scene of fighting and carnage. In 1642, all of Munster save an area around Cork City was controlled by the Confederate Catholics. However, in 1647, Murrough O'Brien, Earl of Inchiquin, leading a Parliamentarian army, soundly defeated their forces at the Battle of Knocknanuss in County Cork. This O'Brien, because of his fierce incendiary reprisals, earned the nickname "Murrogh of the Burnings." One further Parliamentary victory in 1649 paved the way for Cromwell's dreadful march through Ireland, which took him as far into Munster as Glengariff in County Cork; on the way he took Youghal, Cork, Kinsale, and Bandon and on his return eastwards, Waterford, Caher, and Clonmel, leaving death, famine, and disease in his wake.

Ireland represented to Cromwell a means of paying off his debts, mainly arrears of pay to his army and loans raised from adventurers to finance the war campaign. Undesirable or troublesome Irish were deported to the West Indies or transplanted to poor lands west of the Shannon. In Munster, 80 percent of the land in County Clare, 77 percent in County Tipperary, 65 percent in County Cork, 59 percent in County Kerry, 57 percent in County Limerick, and 52 percent in County Waterford was confiscated for Cromwell's use. The confiscated lands in the counties of Limerick, Tipperary, and Waterford were assigned to English adventurers and soldiers, and those in the counties of Clare and Kerry were set aside as an additional security for them. The confiscated lands in County Cork were reserved for the Government. Over one thousand Cromwellian adventurers were recipients of grants, and about thirty-five thousand military, some of whom sold their allotments; it is estimated, however, that about eight thousand settled, radically changing the character of ownership of land in the country. The pattern of Protestant landlord and Catholic tenant or laborer was thus established. Near the end of the seventeenth century with the accession of the Catholic James II, the Catholic Irish had hopes of redress, but there was to be no long-term reversal of the situation because the Jacobites were defeated; their campaign ended in Munster in 1691 with the surrender of Limerick.

At the beginning of the seventeenth century only about 10 percent of the land was in Protestant settler hands; by the end of the century it had increased to 86 percent. A massive redistribution of property had been achieved. After the imposition of the Penal Laws the rift grew even wider; due to the restrictions on Catholic ownership of land, the proportion in Protestant hands reached a staggering 95 percent by the third quarter of the eighteenth century, when Protestants numbered only about 20 percent or less of the whole population in the country at large and only about 10 percent in Munster. A few enlightened men of the favored minority spoke out against this injustice, but most of the landlords were content with their place in the sun.

Munster, with over 90 percent of its population Roman Catholic, reserved practically all the good land, the good houses, and the plum jobs for the Protestant minority, many of whom because of their privileged position were styled gentry. Fifty men, all Protestants, owned one-third of the acreage of County Cork. Much has been written about this class, "the Anglo-Irish," sometimes referred to as "the Ascendancy," and sometimes generically, but incorrectly as "Cromwellians." When Brendan Behan was asked to explain the definition of "Anglo-Irish" he answered, "a Protestant with a horse."

It was not difficult for a Protestant to join the gentry. All he had to do was get enough money together to buy or lease a few acres.

One Munster man who seems to have started life as a Protestant with perhaps little more than a horse, and who rose to the top, was "Copper-faced Jack"; John, son of Thomas Scott of Mohubber, County Tipperary, was born in 1739. He became Attorney-General and Chief Justice of Ireland, and finished his life as Lord Clonmell, having been rewarded with an earldom for his services to the Administration. One contemporary described him as "sporting the ermine on a back that had been coatless, and the Garter glittering on a leg that, in its native bog, had been unencumbered by a stocking." Having acquired property that gave him an income of £20,000 a year, thus making him nearly as rich a magnate as the Earl of Ormonde and the Duke of Leinster, he adopted a suitably haughty manner. Lord Charlemont, in his memoirs, wrote of "Copper-faced Jack," that "he affected to despise that people from whose dregs he had lately sprung, and had indeed an utter contempt for everything, danger only excepted. . . ."

The Anglo-Irish gentry gained a reputation for high-living, hard-drinking, wenching, arrogance, improvidence, and eccentricity. With the exception of a few at the top of the tree, they were not half as grand as they sound. For every devil-may-care buck and gambling rake or rack-renting, spendthrift, libertine landlord, there was a shrewd, temperate, God-fearing farmer, an industrious, honest tradesman, or a small shopkeeper. The officers of the regional militia regiments certainly cut fine figures in their dazzling uniforms, but grand appearances and high-sounding names often went with modest estates.

The residences of the gentry flaunted the often prosaic Anglo-Saxon surnames of their owners. County Limerick boasted Mount Plummer, Mount Brown, Mount Coote, Castle Hewson, Castle Ievers, and Harding's Grove, as well as the more fanciful Fort Etna. Thomas Cooke, a well-to-do Quaker merchant of Cork, gave his name to Castle Cooke in that county where other English settlers loaned their names to such houses as Castle Harrison, Castle Townshend, Castle Bernard, Castle Widenham, Castle Hyde, and Castle Freke, Mount Leader, Mount Rivers, and Mount Long, and the Bowens of Welsh origin built Bowen's Court, described by Elizabeth Bowen. County Tipperary had its Castle Otway, County Waterford its Mount Congreve and Mount Odell, a modest farmhouse. More often than not, the "Castle" was a neat, boxlike Georgian house with no more than eight rooms. Some gentlemen preferred to name their houses for themselves or their wives, hence Palace Anne, Fort Robert and Castle Mary in County Cork, Fortwilliam, Castle Constance, Castle Jane, and Fort Eliza in County Limerick, and Maryfort in County Clare, where the Henn family named their house Paradise Hill. There is a story that an advertisement once appeared announcing that "Mrs. Henn of Paradise has eggs for sale," but the family are no longer there to confirm or deny it. Many of the old settler surnames have vanished, the names of their houses the only reminder of their former presence. Houses still owned and occupied by the families whose names they bear, like the Hewsons at Castle Hewson, are rare. However, the scions of some settler families crossed social and religious boundaries; because of that integration and the issue of back-door relationships, some of the settler names have proliferated. Surnames such as Leader, Bowen, Hyde, and Cudmore can be found today in both churches and in varied walks of life. There has been a considerable mixing of the blood of the English settlers with that of Huguenots from France, Palatines from Germany, and the Hiberno-Norman and the old Irish stock. Inevitably too, some of the old Irish like the Mac Gillycuddys of the Reeks, and the Inchiquin O'Briens, some branches of the MacNamaras and Molonys in County Clare, the Barrys and the Fermoy Roches in County Cork, and some of the hibernicized Norman families like the FitzGeralds, Knights of Kerry, and the FitzGeralds, Knights of Glin, conformed

to the Protestant faith and became a part of Anglo-Irish society in Munster.

Some members of prominent families abused their power and privilege, and did manage to achieve unenviable records of profligacy and extravagant behavior. Inbreeding must have contributed to the outbreaks of eccentricity. In rural Munster, where Protestants were thin on the ground, it was often hard for a young man to find a bride who was not some sort of cousin, and most marriages were arranged within an extended kinship network.

The eccentricity was often manifested in an unusual lifestyle. An astounded English visitor to the Smyths at Ballinatray, County Waterford, reported that she had a horseblanket on her bed, but that the dogs ate from the Capodimonte dish and drank from a Waterford crystal bowl. The dish may have been a memento of Penelope Smyth, who caused an international incident in 1836 by eloping with a Bourbon prince, the brother of the King of Naples and Sicily. The delightful play *Spring Meeting* by Molly Keane was based on her experiences of Anglo-Irish country-house life in Munster. Frequently, the eccentricity was accompanied by lavish overspending, lawsuits, and mortgages, while examples of wild conduct—such as abducting heiresses—were not rare.

In the 1930s, an Anglo-Irish peer with two sons asked an English friend to send his two debutante daughters to stay at his place in County Tipperary, in order, as he put it, "to soften up my boys." The girls were terrified by their host, who chased his wife around the dinner table with a riding crop when she interrupted him. Their hostess devoted most of her day to writing letters of condolence to the families of every single person whose death was announced in the *Irish Times*, regardless of whether she knew them or not. More recently, a guest invited to a black-tie dinner at a mansion in County Cork was greeted by his hostess in long black lace, diamonds, and Wellington boots, and then dispatched to the kitchen to get some brandy for his hostess's large pet bitch, which was pupping on a Chippendale sofa in the drawing room. He found a delicious poached salmon ready on the table, the cook lying stretched drunk on the flagstone floor, and a youth mixing the pigs' food with a fine Georgian silver basting spoon.

The King family, Earls of Kingston, rich and powerful landlords at Mitchelstown, County Cork, where they acquired by marriage the estates of the FitzGibbon family, the White Knights, provide over four generations an exceptional record of unusual behavior. Edward, the first Earl, married the illegitimate daughter of a broguemaker's wife. Their son, Robert, the second Earl, was married at the age of fifteen and began at once to father a family; at the age of twenty-two he had a new mansion built for himself at Mitchelstown. After his father's death in 1797 he became the sixth richest man in Ireland with an income from his estates of £18,000 a year, but by that time his precocious marriage had ended in separation. On finding his daughter Mary in bed in an inn with the married bastard son of his brother-in-law, with whom she had eloped, the Earl shot the seducer dead. He was subsequently tried for murder and acquitted. Mary Wollstonecraft, whom he employed as a governess to his daughters, formed a poor opinion of this second Earl (then Lord Kingsborough) and his wife: "There is such a solemn kind of stupidity about this place as freezes my very blood. Lady Kingsborough is a shrewd, clever woman, a great talker, but her passion for animals fills the hours which are not spent in dressing. She rouges and is, in short, a fine lady, without fancy or sensibility, and I am almost tormented to death with her dogs. I am, however, treated like a gentlewoman by every part of the family, but the forms and parades of high life suit not my mind." Besides Mary, who bolted, the second Earl had a daughter Margaret who married a neighbor, Lord Mount Cashell, but left him and went to live in Italy. There she became a great friend of Shelley, who had married the daughter of her old governess Mary Wollstonecraft; Lady Margaret was "The Lady" in Shelley's *The Sensitive Plant*.

"Big George," the third Earl, eldest son of the second Earl, demolished his father's mansion and built in its stead an immense Gothic Revival castle with towers and fake battlements; it cost him £100,000. He had instructed the architects that he wanted a house bigger than any other in Ireland. The new Mitchelstown Castle was not in fact the largest house in the country but, with its long gallery and grand staircase, it was large enough to appease "Big George"'s appetite for grandeur. The Earl entertained lavishly, his army of domestic servants sometimes waiting on as many as a hundred house guests. One of the Mitchelstown staff, a young assistant cook named Claridge, became the founder of the famous London hotel which bears his name. In 1830 "Big George" summoned his tenants to reprimand them for having voted against his chosen candidate in an election. What happened when they were all assembled is best told by Elizabeth Bowen:

Big George sat on a dais at the far end of the hundred-foot-long castle gallery. As more and more tenants came pressing in at the door, the front of their crowd was pressed more and more up on him. Big George did not cease to cover the mobbed perspective of gallery with his eye. That eye of his, and his dreadful continued silence, renewed the domination of centuries. But they were here to hear him: he must speak. He did not: he took the alternative and went mad. Leaping out of his seat he threw his arms wide. "They are come to tear me to pieces: they are come to tear me, to tear me to pieces!"

Forty-eight hours later he had been taken away.

On the credit side, "Big George" built new churches at Mitchelstown for both the Catholics and Protestants, and he founded almshouses in the town with money from the estate. He epitomized, wrote Elizabeth Bowen, "that rule by force of sheer fantasy that had, in great or small ways, become for his class the only possible one."

"Big George"'s elder son, Edward, Viscount Kingsborough, died before his father. He was an erudite antiquary and edited, in 1831, Aglio's six volumes, *The Antiquities of Mexico.* The younger son, Robert Henry, who succeeded his father as fourth Earl, served as Member of Parliament for County Cork and also entertained on a grand scale, but he ran up heavy debts and had to leave the castle after being besieged by bailiffs. Then in 1848 he was brought before a magistrate in London on a charge of sodomy, but jumped his bail of £10,000. Later, he was frequently in the police courts for drunkenness and insulting behavior. He was declared of unsound mind and was shut up for six years until his death.

Mitchelstown Castle, the pompous mansion of the Earls of Kingston, like many other houses of the settler nobility and gentry, is no more. But the town adjacent to their estate, Mitchelstown, County Cork, laid out by the Earls, survives as a reminder of the family with a splendid main street, fine churches of both denominations, and an elegant square on one side of which are terraced almshouses, a chapel, and a chaplain's house endowed by the landlord for "distressed Protestant gentlefolk." There Miss Travers spent her last years and died, the mysterious woman who claimed to have been seduced by Oscar Wilde's father, Sir William Wilde, and who dragged him through the courts.

A surprising number of the gentry of the new ascendant class lived uncomfortably in tower houses until well into the eighteenth century. Then as they reaped honors and titles they built new residences to reflect their social position.

Bestowing a peerage was a way for the government to repay and to procure loyalty. In the eighteenth century, a great number of Irish peerages were created. In a period of only eighteen days in the summer of 1778, eighteen commoners were raised to the Irish peerage. To force through the Union of England and Ireland, with the consequent abolition of the separate Irish parliament, it was necessary to buy support by distributing more titles. On the eve of the Union thirteen commoners were given peerages, including several Munster landlords. In County Cork, for example, Francis Bernard became Lord Bandon, Richard Longfield became Lord Longueville, and Richard White became Lord Bantry; in County Limerick, William Cecil Pery became Lord Glentworth; and in County Kerry, Sir Valentine Browne became Lord Kenmare. In 1800 a further forty-six Irish peerages were granted to men who had helped push through the Union. Among these also there were a number of prominent Munster landowners: Eyre Massy became Lord Clarina, William Hare became Lord Ennismore, Henry Prittie became Lord Dunally, John Toler became Lord Norbury, Sir Richard Quin became Lord Adare, and Sir Thomas Mullins became Lord Ventry. In subsequent advancements the Hares became Earls of Listowel, the Quins became Earls of Dunraven, the Perys became Earls of Limerick, and the Lords Ventry changed their surname from Mullins to de Moleyns.

Mr. Holmes, an English traveler who published an account of his tour through Munster in 1797, painted an idyllic picture in his *Sketches of Some of the Southern Counties of Ireland*. The Golden Vale of Tipperary, wrote Mr. Holmes, was "a boundless scene of rich cultivation...a tract of country fraught with innumerable beauties, the little village and lordly demesne; the humble cottage and ruined tower; the grove, lawn and rivulet, all in turn court the eye." Adare, in County Limerick, he found "...a serenely beautiful little spot. Silent and retired, its inhabitants few and apparently mixing little with the world." And he was enthusiastic about the surrounding Limerick farmlands: "the soil of this county is of the highest luxuriance and conveys an appearance of fertility delightful to the eye of the traveller. The cornfields and pasture are agreeably varied by extensive cyder orchards, giving, at a distance, all the effect of woodland scenery; and frequently, along the road side, rows of apple-trees cast a cool refreshing shade." Mr. Holmes was no less impressed by Limerick City where he found "the shops elegant and in no way inferior to those of Dublin and London."

Mr. Holmes hoped, he declared in his preface, that on the eve of the Union his work would serve to acquaint English readers with the southwest of Ireland. Occasionally the author found grounds for criticism: at Lismore, which had an absentee landlord, he reported "...a sorry village, some tolerable houses very thinly intermixed with poor cabins." In general his commentary was favorable and his readers could have gained no idea of the misery caused by the system of land tenure in the luxuriant countryside. Land jobbers hired large tracts from the big landlords and let them to tenants, who sublet them in turn to undertenants who had a struggle to survive. Even more wretched and unfortunate were the laborers who received no wages in cash but were paid for their work by plots of land valued far above their actual worth. On these plots the poor would plant a cabbage patch, put down potatoes, perhaps keep a pig, build a windowless cabin, usually of mud. The cost of building a stone cabin with a slated roof was £20 which, if he worked every day of the year, represented over four years of a laborer's wages.

Arthur Young, an English agriculturalist who published the diary of his travels through Ireland between 1776 and 1779 as *A Tour in Ireland*, observed the deplorable conditions in County Kerry:

The state of the poor in the whole county of Kerry represented as exceedingly miserable, and, owing to the conduct of men of property, who are apt to lay the blame on what they call land pirates, or men who offer the highest rent, and who, in order to pay this rent, must, and do re-let all the cabbin lands at an extravagant rise, which is assigning over all the cabbins to be devoured by one farmer. The cottars on a farm cannot go from one to another, in order to find a good master as in England: for all the country is in the same system, and no redress to be found. Such being the case, the farmers are enabled to charge the price of labour as low as they please, and rate the land as high as they like. This is an evil which oppresses them cruelly, and certainly has its origin in its landlords, when they set their farms, setting all the cabbins with them instead of keeping them tenants to themselves. The oppression is, the farmer valuing the labour of the poor at 4d. or 5d. a day, and paying that in land rated much above its value. Owing to this, the poor are depressed; they live upon potatoes and sour milk, and the poorest of them only salt and water to them, with now and then a herring. Their milk is bought; for very few keep cows, scarce any pigs, but a few poultry. Their circumstances are incomparably worse than they were 20 years ago; for they had all cows, but then they wore no linen: all now have a little flax. To these evils have been owing emigrations, which have been considerable.

Like Holmes, Young found Limerick agreeable, "a very gay place, but when the troops are in town even more so." Limerick was expanding rapidly. The population was thirty-two thousand and the cultural amenities included assembly rooms, plays, and concerts. A married gentleman with three children, living in Limerick on an income of £500 per annum, could afford to keep four horses, a carriage and coachman, a butler and two footmen, a cook, a housemaid, a kitchenmaid, and a childrens' nurse. A salmon cost one and a half pence, fine trout two pence a pound, a rabbit four pence, oysters from fourpence a hundred. The kitchenmaid's salary was £2 a year; the professed cook earned six guineas a year.

With these conditions prevailing before the enormous increase in population in the first decades of the last century, it is not surprising that when the potato crop failed in the 1840s the resulting toll was appalling. Following the Act of Union of 1800 and the abolition of the independent Irish Parliament in Dublin, a number of landowners had absented themselves from their Irish estates, spending their time and money in England. Landlords as a class were to reap more of the blame than the greedy middlemen who managed their affairs. Cecil Woodham Smith in her book on the famine years, *The Great Hunger,* wrote of the Irish landlords, "few classes of men have had so much abuse heaped on them...and with justification." Some landowners did try to help and were ruined in the process, others took desperate, drastic, and misguided measures which only brought more opprobrium on their heads. The patriot O'Donovan Rossa, in his reminiscences, recalled a West Cork landlord who, the faster the men, women, and children died each week in the poorhouse, the more he gave thanks to the Lord. Those who died in the poorhouse were luckier than those who died of starvation on the roadsides. Little wonder that the survivors, whether at home in Ireland or emigrés in Canada, the United States, Australia, and England, imparted to their children their hatred of the landlord class.

Only a handful of Catholic families in each of the counties in Munster, like the Wyses in County Waterford and the O'Connells of Derrynane in County Kerry, contrived to remain on a portion of their lands. They had managed to do this either with the complicity of friendly Protestants, or with money from connections in trade in the cities, or from serving in an army on the Continent.

Although the rate of illiteracy was high, over 50 percent, and in Kerry as high as 70 percent, there was a vigorous oral tradition about the hearth. In the twilight of the old Gaelic way of life in the eighteenth century, impoverished poets met in quiet townlands to read their work and encourage one another at Courts of Poetry. In the romantic imagination of the young nineteenth-century poet J. J. Callinan, these last heirs of the bards are pictured gathered at a recital in the hills near Gougane Barra, "in the cleft of thy rocks, and the depth of thy heather." Along with the heroism, the sensitivity and the passion of the early poets, the bawdy earthiness also survived. It is to be found in plenty in *The Midnight Court,* the work of an eighteenth-century schoolmaster in County Clare. It survived into the twentieth century in the stories of the shanachie, the traditional storyteller, and was abundant in the repertoire of the wonderful old storyteller Timothy Buckley of Gougane Barra and his wife, remembered as *The Tailor and Ansty,* the title of the book by Eric Cross. The tailor and his wife considered sexual relations an acceptable and entertaining subject of conversation, but such was the temper of the time that a prudish de Valera government banned the book in 1943 and the poor humiliated tailor was forced to his knees by three bigoted priests who made him burn his own copy of the book in his own hearth. The shame broke the old man and he died soon after. On his grave in the cemetery overlooking the lake at Gougane Barra is Frank O'Connor's epitaph, "A Star Danced and Under that I was Born."

Frank O'Connor's translation of *The Midnight Court* was banned too, but now it has been liberated. Other poets have translated this bawdy poem, among them David Marcus:

The Court considered the country's crisis,
And what do you think its main advice is—
That unless there's a spurt in procreation
We can bid goodbye to the Irish nation;
It's growing smaller year by year—
And don't pretend that's not your affair.
Between death and war and ruin and pillage
The land is like a deserted village;
Our best are banished, but you, you slob,
Have you ever hammered a single job?
What use are you to us, you cissy?
We have thousands of women who'd keep you busy,
With breasts like balloons or small as a bud
Buxom of body and hot in the blood,
Virgins or whores—whatever's your taste—
At least don't let them go to waste;
It's enough to make us broken-hearted—
Legs galore—and none of them parted.
They're ready and willing for any endeavour—
But you can't expect them to wait forever.

Arland Ussher was another of the poets who translated verses of *The Midnight Court*:

For why call a priest in to bind and to bless
Before candid nature can give one caress?
Why lay the banquet and why pay the band
To blow their bassoons and their cheeks to expand?
Since Mary the Mother of God did conceive
Without calling the clergy or begging their leave,
The love-gotten children are famed as the flower
Of man's procreation and nature's power,

Ireland's army of priestly celibates could hardly have liked themselves described as:

Backs erect and huge hind-quarters,
Hot-blooded men, the best of partners,
Freshness and charm, youth and good looks
And nothing to ease their mind but books.

Or an occasional priestly indiscretion recalled:

Many a girl filled byre and stall
And furnished her house through a clerical call.

Early Irish society was seminomadic, and even after its collapse skilled craftsmen like smiths continued to travel about the country offering their services. Before the foundation of urban centers it had been necessary to go looking for work to do. Even after the growth of nucleated settlements, enough of the population was scattered through the rural areas to sustain the practice of itinerant artisans, and there was a market among the farming population for peddlers who offered small household necessities such as needles, tin cups, boot and shoe laces, thread, pins, glassware and china, and also religious pictures and medals and broadsheets with popular ballads. All these needs have been accommodated in recent years by improved transportation and commercial expansion. The settled inhabitants called these traveling people Tinkers; this refers to only one of their crafts, that of mending metal pots and pans. In the eighteenth century the number of these traveling people was increased when rural laborers found themselves without land or employment when their landlords switched from tillage to pasture, and again in the middle years of the last century when more Irish peasants were forced off the land and onto the roads through poverty, famine, and evictions.

Until as late as 1961 over 90 percent of the Irish Tinkers lived in tents or horse-drawn wagons; the barrel-top wagons seen on the roads now, however, were brought to Ireland by Gypsies who came over from England during World War I. There are about ten thousand traveling people in Ireland today. In the last decade a number of families have settled because the services they offered became obsolete, while signing up for and collecting unemployment assistance necessitated some degree of stability of residence. But some Irish Tinkers still prefer the itinerant life and follow their traditional circuits, one of which is a route through North Munster from Limerick up the Shannon and across to Galway, then back through the center of County Clare and Ennis to Limerick; another, all in Munster, covers a route from Killorglin in County Kerry through Tralee, Listowel, and Limerick as far east as Cahir, then via Mitchelstown to Cork, north to Mallow, and west through Killarney to Killorglin.

The nuclear family is the basic social and economic unit in Irish Tinker society, and families that travel together tend to be kinsmen, usually patrilineally related. They have their own secret language known as Gammon or Shelta. Its vocabulary was formerly sufficient to express the needs of their everyday existence, but now most travelers have a vocabulary of only about one hundred and fifty words of Gammon, useful for exchanging advice, for example, in the course of horse-dealing with an outsider, or to give a word of warning secretly. Philologists have not been able to deduce the origin of Gammon, which includes such words as *gropa* (shop), *glox* (boss or landowner), *beor* (woman), and *tober* (road).

Travelers of another sort, tourists, come in great numbers to Munster, and they too have their circuit, which usually includes Killarney. Munster's most famous tourist attraction is so splendid that the proximity of the town, which grows steadily more unattractive, has done little to put off visitors, who continue to be enchanted by the magnificent scenery and wooed by a sweetness that has survived the passage of time.

At the end of the eighteenth century Mr. Holmes described the town of Clonmel, County Tipperary, in glowing terms: "The people are wealthy, the happy consequence of industry, which here has been manifested by the people called Quakers, who from their first settling in this town have gradually added to its trade, having introduced the woollen manufacture and still continue it. There is the most pleasing appearance of cleanliness through the town, even to its suburbs." Happily many more small towns in Munster now have this air of prosperity and cleanliness. The land is more equitably distributed, and if the exigencies of industrial progress have reduced the Falls of Doonass to a shadow of their former splendor, if the flush of consumer-society prosperity has spoiled the gracious aspect of Limerick City, and if the Blaskets have lost their inhabitants, whose way of life was so finely described by Robin Flower and by their own Peig Sayers and Thomas O'Crohan, then also the people of Munster are better housed and better clad, the flow of emigration has been stanched, and the future looks bright.

The author of *A Week in the South of Ireland*, who published his book under the pseudonym of "An Old Traveler," wrote in his introduction observations and recommendations which are as good today as when they were made in 1852:

It would be difficult to discover within the British Isles any district where the tourist can more agreeably occupy himself for a week or two in summer or autumn than in the South of Ireland. The facilities for traversing the localities to which we shall allude, are at present so admirable that the toil of travel is just sufficient to enhance its pleasure and brace the frame...take with you a light cape, strong shoes, a stout stick, a large map, a small land compass and a leather flask, and you are armed to the teeth.

Munster now has two international airports: Cork, with connections to Britain and Continental Europe, and Shannon, with transatlantic connections as well. An ever-increasing number of visitors fly in each year, drive around, admire, and leave, sometimes with scarcely more time than to crane their necks at Cashel or gasp at the beauty of Killarney's lakes and mountains and moss-clad oaks, before they are whisked away. The Cork Film Festival now attracts many visitors to that city, and those who take the time to travel by boat can be delighted by the magnificent approach to the harbor. But the visitor who really wants to savor the loveliness of Munster must use his feet. Roam along the cliffs from Ardmore to Whiting Bay, climb in the Knockmealdowns or the Comeraghs, wander down the country lanes or along the riverbanks, lean over a medieval bridge, rove on Mizen Head, walk along the cliffs of the Dingle peninsula where Minnaunmore, which escaped the glaciers, interrupts the skyline with its serrated silhouette, gaze across to the dark purple sandstone pinnacles and precipitous stacks of the Blaskets and to the Three Sisters, where the sea has encroached through a ridge of old red sandstone to create the expanse of Smerwick harbor in the vale and works inexorably to isolate Sybil Head and make another island. That is the way to fall in love with the land and feel its sweetness, its roughness, and its strange, sad past of lust and love and laughter and tears.

opposite: *Cove near Clogher Head, Dingle Peninsula, County Kerry. J.M. Synge wrote of the "severe glory" of this landscape.*

above and below: *Ferriter's Cove, County Kerry.*

following spread: *The limestone mass of the Rock of Cashel, which rises dramatically above the plain of County Tipperary, was the seat of pagan monarchs before Christianity came to Ireland. The ruins date from Christian times when Cashel became an important ecclesiastical center—the See of an archbishop since 1152. The rectangular tower and steeply-pitched roofs of the richly decorated Romanesque church, Cormac's Chapel, were built between 1127 and 1134 by king Cormac MacCarthy. The Round Tower was built about the same time. In the fifteenth century, Gerald FitzGerald set fire to the adjacent thirteenth-century cathedral because, as he said, he thought the Archbishop was inside.*

above: *Fuchsia has run wild in Ireland, especially in the southwest, where miles of brilliant hedgerows grow.*

opposite: *Wooden footbridge, Gougane Barra, County Cork.*

following spread: *The spectacular Cliffs of Moher tower more than two hundred meters above the Atlantic along five miles of the coast of County Clare, between Hag's Head and O'Brien's Tower.*

above: *Detail of eighth-century High Cross, Ahenny, County Tipperary.*

left: *Curiously painted shopfront in Sneem, County Kerry.*

following spread: *"Ladies View" from the Kenmare Road, so named, perhaps, because the ladies of Queen Victoria's retinue stopped here to admire the view over the Killarney lakes, with Eagle's Nest on the left and Torc Mountain on the right.*

above: *Lobster pots, Ballynagaul, County Waterford.*

left: *Turf-cuttings in blanket bog, Ballinskelligs, County Kerry.*

At Dromana, County Waterford, a rare example of the exotic Hindu–Gothic style immortalized by the Prince Regent at the Royal Pavilion, Brighton. In 1826, the tenants of Henry Villiers-Stuart of Dromana erected a gateway at the bridge over the River Finisk, to greet their landlord and his bride upon their return from their honeymoon. So delighted was the couple that they made it into a permanent structure to serve as a gatehouse.

Dancing maidens, after nineteenth-century originals by Canova, in the gardens of Bantry House, above Bantry Bay. Once the residence of the Earls of Bantry, the house, still owned by their descendants, is open to the public.

above, left: *The South Cross, one of two elaborately carved High Crosses at Ahenny, County Tipperary, believed to date from the eighth century and among the earliest examples in the country.*

above, top right: *A Paleo-Christian cross beside Gallarus Oratory on the Dingle Peninsula, County Kerry.*

above, bottom right: *At Nenagh, County Tipperary, two mothers sit and chat with their children on the steps of a large cross of Celtic inspiration erected to commemorate a local prelate.*

opposite: *The ruins of the best-preserved stone fort in the country, dating from the first centuries of our era, in an isolated valley at Staigue, County Kerry. The interior enclosure of the fort, nearly twenty-eight meters in diameter, is reached by a passage. The walls measure more than four meters at their thickest and about five-and-a-half meters at their highest.*

above: *The jaunting car is popular along the shores of the Lakes of Killarney, where the best drives are closed to motor vehicles. The car drivers, or jarveys, have a large repertoire of tall tales.*

opposite, top: *Shopfront, Clonmel, County Tipperary. The bar and grocery are built into the Main Guard, a handsome building erected in the seventeenth century to house the main guard of the garrison. It later served as the Tholsel, or Town Hall.*

opposite, bottom left: *Market day, Kenmare, County Kerry. Cattle at the crossroads.*

opposite, bottom right: *Early nineteenth-century house-shop at Ballingarry, County Limerick. Such shopfronts, the work of local artisan-designers, add a distinctive elegance to many Irish towns and villages. Unfortunately, they are fast disappearing.*

opposite: *The "soporific lime walk," in the now-neglected gardens of Doneraile Court, County Cork, described by Elizabeth Bowen.*

below: *St. Patrick's Well and the ruined medieval church near Clonmel, County Tipperary.*

above: *Slabs of the limestone pavement of the Burren have been stacked to form these walls that mark a little track. The hardy hawthorn grows in an almost treeless area. Such isolated trees were frequently regarded as fairy thorn trees by the country people.*

opposite: *Old Head of Kinsale, County Cork.*

above: *Nineteenth-century estate house, Castle Bernard, Bandon, County Cork.*

opposite: *A traveling family camped on the roadside in Munster. The Irish itinerants, long known as Tinkers, are so named for one of their trades. They are often fair-complexioned, unlike the itinerant Romany people or gypsies of Britain and continental Europe.*

following spread: *This stone circle at Drombeg, County Cork, consisting of seventeen standing stones, dates from about the time of Christ. Remains of a cremation burial were found in the center of the circle.*

Clogher Head, Dingle Peninsula, County Kerry. opposite: *Minnaunmore Rock;* above and below: *Rock plants.*

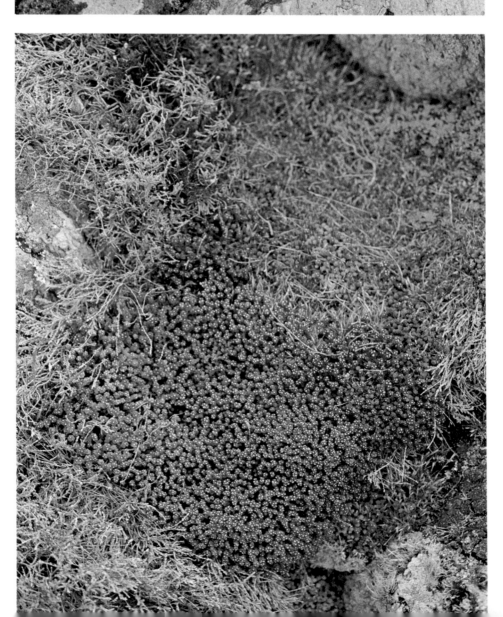

opposite: *Sheep graze peacefully beneath the ruins of Ballynalackan Castle in the Barony of Corcomroe, County Clare. The medieval castle was repaired in the last century by John O'Brien of Elm Vale.*

below: *Market day at Kenmare, County Kerry.*

preceding spread: *The currach or* naomhoge, *a light but sturdy canoe constructed of tarred fabric over a framework of wicker or wooden laths, is still used in rough seas on the Atlantic coast of Ireland. This upturned currach, with its propitiatory bottle of holy water attached, is weighted down against the wind and lies in a cove beneath Sybil Head, Dingle Peninsula, County Kerry.*

opposite: *Caha Mountains, County Cork.*

below: *Gorse, Caha Mountains.*

Connacht

"For peace comes dropping slow"

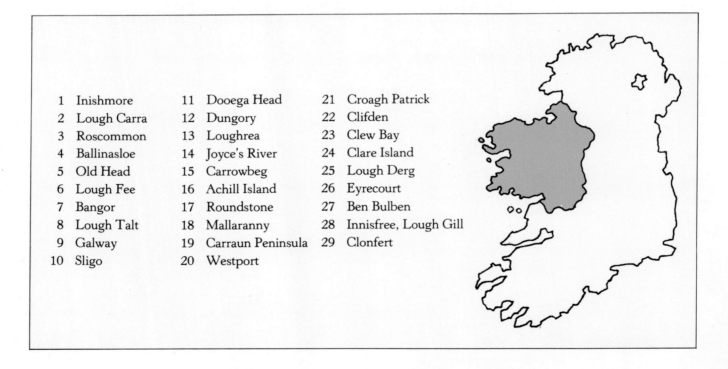

1	Inishmore	11	Dooega Head	21	Croagh Patrick
2	Lough Carra	12	Dungory	22	Clifden
3	Roscommon	13	Loughrea	23	Clew Bay
4	Ballinasloe	14	Joyce's River	24	Clare Island
5	Old Head	15	Carrowbeg	25	Lough Derg
6	Lough Fee	16	Achill Island	26	Eyrecourt
7	Bangor	17	Roundstone	27	Ben Bulben
8	Lough Talt	18	Mallaranny	28	Innisfree, Lough Gill
9	Galway	19	Carraun Peninsula	29	Clonfert
10	Sligo	20	Westport		

preceding spread: *Glenade Lough, County Leitrim.*

When people in Ireland speak of "The West" or "the West of Ireland," they could, of course, be referring to any of the western part of the island, from Donegal in the northwest to the extremities of West Cork in the southwest. Invariably they are referring to Connacht, and usually they have in mind its three Atlantic seaboard counties, Galway, Mayo, or Sligo — the "West" that has a special glamor of its own. The sublime beauty of the Connemara scenery with its tawny browns, pearly grays, muted violets, and misty blues, created by the luminescent Atlantic light, is now a tourist attraction second only to Killarney; there is the glamor of the Gaeltabht with its smooth-tongued native Irish speakers; there is the glamor of the vanishing way of life in rural Connacht; there is the glamor of the province's role in the Celtic Revival.

To say that Connacht is the most Irish part of the country, or that it is more Irish than the other provinces, is to subscribe to the untenable theory that only one strand of Ireland's broad cultural inheritance is truly Irish. It is true, however, that for geographical and historical reasons, the five Connacht counties, Galway, Mayo, Sligo, Leitrim and Roscommon, less subject to outside influences, have been a harbinger of a way of life that in the other three provinces has been greatly eroded.

The northern boundary of Connacht is the northern boundary of County Leitrim, north of its narrow three-mile seaboard where the county border marches with that of Donegal, then along its border with Ulster. To the east Connacht has a natural frontier, the Shannon, Ireland's longest river, which rises at the Shannon Pot, an insignificant pool on a boulder-strewn slope of the Cuilcagh Mountains; but once Connacht extended beyond the Shannon far into Cavan. For about one hundred years, Clare, to the south of the present province, was detached from Munster and joined to Connacht. The geological, variety of Connacht is second only to that of Ulster; the glorious mountains, lakes, and rivers, the desolate bogland, the rugged coastline, with its islands, give the province a variety second to none.

Along the north shore of Galway Bay an outcrop of Paleozoic granite stretches from Bertraghboy Bay as far as the city of Galway, forming the low, gently rolling hills of Iar Connacht, physically subdued by the high Pre-Cambrian quartzite peaks of the Maumturk Mountains and the Twelve Pins of Connemara. To the east the granite descends beneath the carboniferous limestone of the Corrib country, but along the coastal margin where it is on the surface, the fields are so stony and the grass so scant that J.M. Synge commented that the very thought of tillage in the small plots seemed like the freak of an eccentric. Nevertheless Iar Connacht supports a surprisingly large population, whose poor agricultural income is supplemented by home industries such as knitting and making tweed, and by fishing which, on this coast, where the Atlantic swell can so easily dash a boat to pieces against a submerged rock, is difficult and dangerous.

North of Connemara on the borders of County Galway and County Mayo, and less well known to the tourist, is some of the finest mountain scenery in Connacht: deep valleys, waterfalls, corrie lakes in mountainside hollows, and the mountains of the Kilbride ridge, which divides the two southern arms of Lough Mask, the wooded slopes reflected in its bright waters. County Mayo has, altogether, a varied topography: the gritstone Sheefry Hills and Mweelrea Mountains in the west, with Mweelrea, Connacht's highest peak, the isolated beauty of Croaghpatrick's quartzite peak which towers 2,317 meters over the drowned drumlin landscape of Clew Bay, the treeless moorland of Achill and its splendid peaks, Slievemore and Croaghaun, both over 2,000 meters. The massive quartzite mountains of North Mayo guard the shapely peak of Nephin Beg, which rises above a thousand square kilometers of treeless blanket bog in Erris, undoubtedly the least frequented area in Ireland. There are lush farmlands and meadows east of Crossmolina between Lough Conn and Killala Bay and then south and east of Foxford, the dull, featureless limestone Mayo Plains.

Westport, County Mayo, at the eastern end of Clew Bay, is the most elaborately planned of the smaller towns of Ireland, a fine example of town planning long before environmentalists became concerned with urban layout. The local landlords, the Brownes, now Marquesses of Sligo, hoped that Westport would become the major port for the north of Connacht, but any maritime importance it may have enjoyed is gone, the warehouses on the quays are empty, and now only small coastal vessels are to be seen in the harbor. The town was laid out in 1780 when the dream of development was vivid, with a spacious octagonal market place, now daubed with slogans like "BRITS OUT," an elegant mall lined with rows of lime trees, and the neat stone bridges over the canalized Carrowbeg River, which flows out into the bay through the town and through the fine, well-timbered demesne of Westport House, seat of the Lords Sligo. In the center of the Octagon is a gaunt octagonal pedestal and plinth, all that remains of a statue erected in 1843 to commemorate George Clendenning, a native of Westport who ran the local bank and died in that year. In 1916, British troops billeted in Westport took potshots at the statue. Then during the Civil War in 1922–3 the head was smashed to splinters. In 1943, some patriotic inhabitants of Westport, inspired by the removal of some statues in the capital, arranged the dismantling of the headless Mr. Clendenning. A recent report on Westport and its environs recommends the renovation of the Octagon and the restoration of the statue. Local opinion is divided. Some welcome the return of Mr. Clendenning; others would prefer a statue of a Westport man who distinguished himself by fighting with the Boers against the British in the South African War; some want a statue of Christ the King; others an avant-garde symbolic bronze figure looking into the future.

In 1842, the year before the death of the controversial Mr. Clendenning, the English novelist, William Makepeace Thackeray, visited and admired Westport on his tour of Ireland. In *The Irish Sketch Book*, published in 1843, Thackeray exclaimed at the beauty of Clew Bay, "the most beautiful view I ever saw in the world... A miracle of beauty" and continued his description "... the Bay, the Reek, which sweeps down to the sea, and a hundred islands in it, were dressed up in gold and purple, and crimson, with the whole cloudy West in a flame."

"The Reek" to which Thackeray refers is the local name of Croaghpatrick, Patrick's Reek, the "Holy Mountain" on which Saint Patrick is believed to have fasted for forty days and nights. According to legend, it was at the summit that Patrick banished the snakes from Ireland. Every year, on the last Sunday of July, formerly on Garland Friday, pilgrims toil up the steep rough track which winds to the top of Croaghpatrick. Although the climb is arduous and the sharp rocks lacerate all but the stoutest footwear, fifty thousand or more pilgrims annually make the ascent and, as a further penance, a few even go barefoot. The procession makes fifteen circuits around the chapel on the summit, seven circuits round each of two other stations on the route, and seven around each of three mounds at a third station.

Rivaling Westport's claim to fame for its elegant town plan is Ballina, County Mayo, which has gained a reputation as one of the two best market towns in Ireland, reflecting the prosperity of the region, the best farmland in the county. The cattle, the horses, the donkeys, the mules, and the vegetable-laden carts which once crowded the flagstoned streets of Ballina on Mondays have gone, as have the ass-drawn carts which used to line up along the riverside,

and the countrymen who sealed their bargains with a spit on the palm and the exchange of a good-luck coin, and who washed the deal down with bellyfuls of whiskey and porter. Gone sadly also are the threshing masses of salmon; the Ridge Pool of the Moy River was reputed to be the richest salmon stretch in all of Ireland or Britain but now the Moy is a dirty brown and the salmon are not tempted to come up river from the Atlantic to their old breeding grounds. Ballina's flagstones have been replaced by smooth concrete, and if the salmon have been lost with the overhasty drainage of the Moy, on the positive side, industry — a Japanese synthetic fiber factory, an American hospital-supplies factory, a toy factory, and a tool factory — has helped to banish the grinding poverty of the town's many unemployed and slow the rate of emigration, long the bane of the West, where Nancy Mitford observed that the busiest shops were those that sold cardboard suitcases.

Castlebar, County Mayo, has undergone an even more radical change than Ballina. The population has doubled in the last ten years and the growth is expected to continue. The American-owned Travenol Laboratories alone now employs about 1,000 women and 250 men, whereas in the mid-1960s less than 100 women and only 250 men were employed in industry in the whole town. Traffic now jams the streets; the town's infrastructure is severely strained. The sawdust and spit has gone from the floors of the public houses which only twenty years ago were strictly a male preserve, and some bars are now frequented by the working girls. In this new affluence the ten thousand Roman Catholics of Castlebar are collecting money to help the twenty-two Protestants to repair the roof of the Church of Ireland church.

At Louisburgh, County Mayo, the May fair retains some of its old bustle and panache. It can be heartrending to watch the dealers there bargain with the Clare Islanders for their ewes and lambs. The hardy islanders have to bring their sheep over on the day before the fair or even earlier if the weather is unsettled, coping with the difficult crossing with their sheep in small vessels. The mainland buyers know that the islanders will not want to take their ewes back so they ignore them where they cluster together, not approaching them with an offer until the end of the day when they will be able to get the islanders to accept a low price in order to get off home.

While new industry is changing some of the towns of Connacht, ecological changes and increased tourism are changing some of the more accessible scenic areas. When the English botanist Edward Newman visited Achill in 1838 he wrote: "...Achill is more like a foreign land than any I have visited; the natives reside in huts, which a good deal resemble those of the Esquimaux Indians; they are without chimneys or window..." and of Bunnafreeva Lough "I doubt whether any Englishman but myself has ever seen this lone and beautiful sheet of water. ..." Happily, nobody in Connacht now lives in a windowless, chimneyless cabin, and travelers from many countries will have seen Bunnafreeva, but sadly the White-tailed Sea Eagle, which Newman reported to be abundant, is now extinct in Ireland. Achill's main charm, according to the Ulster naturalist Dr. Robert Lloyd Praeger who first went there in 1898, was what he termed its "unchanging features ... the broad undulations of the treeless, roadless moorland, the tall hills, the illimitable silver sea, the savage coast-line, the booming waves, the singing wind, the smell of peat smoke and seaweed and Wild Thyme, and the soft western voices bidding you welcome or giving you God-speed."

Some of the "unchanging features" have changed since Praeger wrote that in 1937. Miles of modern road now cross the "roadless" moorland; caravans, bungalows, hotels and restaurants dot the "savage" coastline, but the hills are still tall and the sea still silver, the waves still boom and the wind sings; there are fewer turf fires and less wild thyme to blend their unique scents, and some of the "soft western voices" now announce the price of knickknacks in the gift shops or betray their owners' years of temporary exile in London or Hoboken or Seattle. But for the urban man this part of the West is still paradise. And if he will venture a little off the tarmac road he may feel as if time stands still.

Whether Edward Newman was the first Englishman to see Lough Bunnafreeva or not, it is true that few outsiders explored the remoter west of Connacht before the last century. As Beaufort's Map of Ireland of 1792 showed no roads at all in Connemara, the paucity of visitors then is not surprising. Much interest in the region was stimulated by a book published by John Murray in London in 1825, *Letters from the Irish Highlands*. It consisted of letters describing life there, written by members of the Blake family of Renvyle, County Galway, and principally by Henry Blake, who decided about 1816 to move to his estate there and take it out of the hands of a middleman.

Mr. Blake loved the scenery of Connacht. When he reached Lough Corrib he wrote, "the sunrise over Lough Corrib is one of the finest scenes imaginable, the lough to the south as smooth as glass." He also had a warm sympathy for the Connemara people, was tolerant of what he considered their shortcomings, and quick to praise their skill and zeal. Henry Blake dismissed cases of laziness as "the vice of contentment." In one letter he writes, "... there is a delicacy of feeling amongst the lower orders of the Irish not generally to be met with in the same rank in England." In another letter he asks the recipient to "... remember that the family of an Irish peasant without wages or employment, living on the produce of their few potatoe beds, must needs find as much difficulty in scraping together a few tenpennies, as your English labourer, who receives his wages every Saturday night, would find in collecting as many pounds. The money that the poor women gain by their knitting, which with those who devote much time to it, does not exceed one shilling per week, is required for many uses."

Mr. Blake's sympathy and concern for the country people led him to criticize what he deemed the avarice of the priests, who depended for their stipends on fees exacted for administering the sacraments. Baptism was free, but it was usually performed when the mother was churched, a ceremony which cost three shillings and four pence. Extreme unction, the anointing of the sick, cost two shillings and sixpence, and a marriage cost from one guinea to one pound and ten shillings, plus a further guinea for a dispensation on the grounds of consanguinity, which was frequently needed. He also deplored some of the superstitions that he felt were encouraged, such as the wearing of charms against sickness, commonly called "Gospels," which the poor people purchased and wore. One of these, described in the Blake letters, was a cloth bag marked IHS; it contained a piece of paper with on one side the Lord's Prayer and on the other the following curious handwritten text which is quoted verbatim:

> In the name of God Amen. When our Saviour
> saw the cross whereon he was To Be Crucified
> his body trembiled and shook the Jews asked
> Iff he had the faver or the ague he said
> that he had neither the faver or the ague.
> Whosoever shall keep these words in mind
> or in righting shall never have the faver
> or the ague. Be the hearers Blessed. Be the
> Believers Blessed. Be the name of our Lord god
> Amen
>
> Cy Toole

Henry Blake also recorded numerous conversations with

country people. Once, congratulating a girl about to be married, he told her that a good husband was a great blessing. He realized immediately that his comment was trite. Not so the delightful answer of the girl, "It is a blessing if it please God, to find a shelter from every wave."

The letters admit that life at Renvyle was "not without privations," but Mr. Blake proclaimed that their life style was that of the "old feudal Barons ... cut off from the ordinary routine of society ... enjoying in proud solitude the grandeur of our rocks and mountains, surrounded by warm-hearted faithful dependants and with no rival chieftain within a distance of fifteen miles." These were heady words to readers accustomed to the romantic novels of Sir Walter Scott.

Among those attracted to western Galway and Mayo by the Blakes' descriptions of life there was the novelist Maria Edgeworth. While writing that it was "a part of Ireland which from time immemorial I had been curious to see," she admitted that her curiosity had been aroused by reading the *Letters from the Irish Highlands*. In a letter to her youngest brother, then in India, Miss Edgeworth left a long account of her expedition, which began from her home in County Longford in 1833. It was partially published in 1867 as *Tour in Connemara* but not published in full until 1950. Although Maria Edgeworth was not insensitive to natural beauty there is barely any description of the scenery in her travelogue, her deeper interest being, as she wrote, "the ways of life so different from any other part of Ireland." Her adventure, she felt, began at the very gates of Connacht, getting out of Athlone through the entrance to the narrow old-fashioned bridge over the Shannon. The carriage was wedged in and blocked by drays and sheep stretching for at least a mile, the men cursing in Irish and in English, the shepherds brandishing their crooks, and the postillions lashing the sheep with their whips.

At Ballinasloe in County Galway, Miss Edgeworth and her English traveling companions, Sir Culling and Lady Smith, were advised to go very quietly through the town as there was a local superstition that no woman should be seen at the Ballinasloe fair, so any woman seen out could be in imminent peril from the mob. The travelers were told that the daughters of Lord Clancarty, who resided at Garbally, a mansion on the edge of the town, had once tried to venture out during the fair and were saved from the mob in the nick of time. Miss Edgeworth and the Smiths stayed comfortably at the Protestant Rectory. On reaching Oughterard, however, they began to suffer from the lack of facilities for travelers. The only inn was execrable and they were unable to find lodging with the priest or a local official. Eventually they were taken in as paying guests in a small private house where the sons of the family were ejected from their beds to make room for them. Miss Edgeworth may have reflected on Henry Blake's description of local hospitality when he came to Lough Corrib a few years earlier and was entertained by the most prominent inhabitant of the region, the local Justice of the Peace, Anthony O'Flaherty. The "Big House" of Mr. O'Flaherty was a thatched dwelling, one story high, about sixty feet in length by twenty wide, with an eating parlor and a sitting room off each of which opened two small bedrooms. Bagpipers played throughout the copious meal, which included a fine dish of sea kale. After dinner the visitors, the family, and the local priests enjoyed plenty of duty-free wines and spirits.

It is not without interest to compare that account of O'Flaherty hospitality with an account of over a century earlier. John Dunton, a London bookseller who visited Ireland about 1699, prepared for publication his travelogue entitled *Teague Land, or a Merry Ramble to the Wild Irish*. Dunton ventured as far as Iar Connacht, which he found very different from the other parts of the country, describing it as "a wild mountainous country in which the old barbarities of the Irish are so many and so common that untill I came hither I lookt for Ireland in itself to no purpose." What he referred to as "barbarities" were actually innocuous practices which seemed horribly outmoded to him such as grinding oats with a quern or churning with the naked hand instead of a churnstaff. Dunton had a recommendation to the O'Flaherty chieftain whom he found in residence at his summer habitation, a booley, where the Englishman was received most hospitably, being provided with "sheets and soft white blankets while everyone else lay on green rushes which were changed each day." This superior booley was a long cabin with walls made of hurdles plastered with clay and thatched with rushes or coarse grass. Inside there was one long room which had a central fire and a vent hole for the smoke. For dinner, a whole beef, as well as lots of mutton, and three foot-high piles of oaten cakes were served. As well as ale, which Dunton found bad, and aqua vitae, there were two large vessels filled with "troander," a beverage of whey made with buttermilk and sweet milk, of which Dunton wrote, "being about two days old it was wonderfull cold and pleasing in the hott time of day."

As O'Flaherty's family, clansmen, and guests were at the

house, Dunton was able to observe them and the customs which were unusual to him. The men he described as "tall lusty fellows with long haire, straite and well made, only clumsy in their leggs, their ankles thicker in proportion to their calves than the English which is attributed to their weareing broags without any heels." He noticed that the men "after the old Irish fashion," as well as the women, wore their hair "verie long as an ornament" and reported of the women's way of dressing their hair, "... the women, commonly on Saturday night or the night before they make theire appearance at mass or any publick meeting do wash it in a lie made with stale urine and ashes, and after in water to take away the smell; by which their locks are of a burnt yellow colour much in vogue among them."

Dunton was most impressed, however, by the O'Flaherty's wolfhounds. "One thing I saw in this house, perhaps the like not to be seen anywhere else in the world," he wrote, "and that was nine brace of Wolfe doggs ... a pair of which kind has been often a present for a king as they are said to be a dog that is peculiar to Ireland." The O'Flahertys informed their visitor that the dogs earned their keep by the number of deer they killed. Dunton was full of admiration for the great hounds but relieved when he found that at night they slept in their own kennel, a cabin specially prepared for them. When he went hunting in Glenglass with the O'Flaherty men, the hounds caught a large stag and he was then able to observe how well trained and obedient they were.

One of Miss Edgeworth's hosts in the West was Mr. Martin of Ballynahinch, called the "King of Connemara." According to the novelist he was a large, powerful man, whom she liked but described as "coarsish," mentioning that he spoke with a "Connemara brogue." She remarked too on "his brusque cordiality," which she explained as "the Connemara manner." Mrs. Martin was gentle and kind; the only child, Miss Martin, the "Princess of Connemara," was clever but eccentric. Mr. Martin managed his vast estate from his seat, Ballynahinch Castle, on the lake of the same name, dominated by the Twelve Pins. The Edgeworth party arrived unexpectedly at the Castle, which Miss Edgeworth thought had "nothing of a castle about it," very tired and badly shaken by their journey in an unsuitable carriage over appalling roads. Time and again their carriage had to be hoisted out of deep sloughs by a train of country fellows who followed it for that purpose, and it nearly broke. In despair, Miss Edgeworth sent a lad to run with her card to the Martins who at once invited her to stay.

The Martins were incredibly hospitable, even to unknown travelers through Connemara, although Mrs. Martin's patience was tried by one bumptious young English gentleman who asked her, "Have you had many travellers here this season?" She turned to Miss Edgeworth and said, "As if I kept an Inn!"

At Ballynahinch, Maria Edgeworth found the fare excellent, she remarked that the Martins had their own deer island and their own private oyster bed, but she did not fail either to report that her bedchamber, though spacious, was scantily furnished and without curtains. The drawing room lacked curtains too and the shutters rattled, but Miss Edgeworth found it tolerably well furnished; she admired the magnificent mahogany doors but complained that they fitted badly. Soon after their arrival Lady Culling Smith fell ill with a crippling attack of gout, so the whole party was obliged to stay for three weeks. During this time the Martins never flinched nor failed in their gracious hospitality, even though the guests were strangers. This long unplanned stay was an advantage to Maria Edgeworth — as Lord Sligo subsequently pointed out to her — providing, as it did, time to observe life in Connemara. She was impressed by the feudal life style and wrote that the people looked on Mr. Martin as the "Lord of their lives." As there was no doctor for many miles he and his daughter were accustomed to tend the sick and prescribe for them; the postal service added to their isolation because letters were carried three times a week from Clifden to Oughterard. Three lads ran the distance; one ran for a day and a night then slept while another took his turn leaping over the hills with his leather bag. For this the boys were paid fifteen pounds per annum.

A few years after Maria Edgeworth's tour Mr. Martin contracted the Famine fever while visiting sick tenants in Clifden workhouse, and his estate was sold up by the Encumbered Estates Court to cover the debts originally incurred by his father, Richard Martin, known as "Humanity Dick" because of his concern for animal welfare. That extravagant man once boasted to King George IV that his Connemara estate was so vast that the approach from his gatehouse to his hall was thirty miles long. After her father's death and the sale which left her homeless, the "Princess of Connemara" emigrated to the United States. In this century Ballynahinch Castle was bought by a world-famous sportsman and cricket champion, the Maharajah Jam Saheb of Nawanagar, popularly called "Ranji," of whom Tim Healey, the first Governor-General of the Irish Free State, said, "He might have fished in the Ganges but he prefers the river at Ballynahinch." The castle is now a hotel with twenty bedrooms.

Elegant Westport House in County Mayo where Maria Edgeworth and the Culling Smiths stayed in comfort as guests of Lord Sligo at the end of their tour, and where Miss Edgeworth was delighted to see a park with trees and shrubberies again, has been opened to the public by the Earl of Altamont, the son of the present Marquess of Sligo.

The Blakes' house, Renvyle, overlooking the Atlantic at the western end of Connemara, was eventually purchased by Oliver St. John Gogarty, the urbane and witty Dublin surgeon who also achieved some renown as a writer. The sale seems to have included a Blake ghost, and Gogarty and his guests were frequently troubled by supernatural phenomena. Once when the door of the haunted north room on the upper floor could not be opened, workmen who climbed up from outside and sawed through the bars of the window to enter, found that a heavy chest had been mysteriously moved up against the door on the inside. In 1917, when William Butler Yeats and his bride were staying with Gogarty on their honeymoon, they conducted a seance with Lord Conyngham and another guest in an attempt to communicate with the ghost. Yeats ordered it to desist from frightening children in their first sleep, to stop moaning about the chimneys, walking about the house, or moving furniture; lastly he commanded it to tell its name. Meanwhile, young Evan Morgan, later Lord Tredegar, was locked in the haunted room by Seymour Leslie, today a spritely ninety-year-old and the only survivor of that house party. The young man came out so badly frightened that some of the guests thought he was dying. When he had sufficiently recovered from his shock he explained that a pale-faced boy with large luminous brown eyes and dressed in brown velvet had appeared to him, and then went through the motions of strangling himself, indicating that he had committed suicide in that room. Mrs. Yeats then took a spell alone in the same room. She came calmly from her vigil to tell her husband what she had seen. Yeats informed the other guests that a pallid red-haired boy of about fourteen named "Athalstone Blake," had appeared to his wife. But either the ghost was confused about his name or Mrs. Yeats was, or Gogarty's memory was faulty when he wrote of these shenanigans. "Athalstone" can be identified with an Ethelstane Blake, but he lived to be fifty-eight, married, and left children of his own. It was this Ethelstane's older brother Ethelred Blake who died aged 14 in 1838, who would have been the boy who died in the house. One can understand the confusion, for Henry Blake had the humor to name his seven sons Edgar Henry, Harold Henry, Ethelbert Henry, Egbert Henry, Ethelred Henry, Ethelstane Henry, and Herbert Henry.

Sadly, Renvyle House was burned by the I.R.A. during the Civil War. In his memoirs, *As I Was Walking Down Sackville Street*, published in 1937, Gogarty recalled the happy years in his "long lone house in the ultimate land of the undiscovered West." Lovingly he had written of Renvyle in its heyday when he entertained there lavishly, that it "stands on a lake, but it stands also on the sea. Water-lilies meet the golden seaweed. It is as if, in the faery land of Connemara at the extreme end of Europe, the incongruous flowed together at last; and the sweet and bitter blended. Behind me, islands and mountainous mainland share in a final reconciliation at this, the world's end." After the house was destroyed Gogarty, reminiscing, remembered among his guests at Renvyle the long, nervous hands of the painter Augustus John and the psychic experiences of the Yeatses. Gogarty eventually rebuilt the bare ruin "on Europe's extreme edge" as an hotel, which it still is today.

Many literary guests stayed at Renvyle, but the undoubted literary center of Connacht for three decades was in a less remote part of County Galway, the Barony of Kiltartan, where Lady Gregory was hostess at Coole Park to Yeats, Synge, Shaw, Hyde, Masefield, George Moore, Sean O'Casey, and many other brilliant men. Born Augusta Persse of Roxboro' House, County Galway, Lady Gregory came to Coole Park in 1880 as the bride of its owner, Sir William Gregory. Before their marriage, he had written to her of the tenants on his estate. "They have never in a single instance caused me displeasure, and I know you can and will do everything in your power to make them love and value us." Years later, Lennox Robinson wrote of Lady Gregory, "... she was an Irish Protestant but impatient with Irish Protestantism because her heart was with the people. Although she worshipped every Sunday in Gort Parish Church her heart was across the road. ..." Across the road was the Catholic Church, the place of worship of the country people whom Lady Gregory loved and from whom she learned old Connacht lore. She drove in her phaeton across the Galway mountains, often with Yeats and Douglas Hyde, on expeditions which she called "folkloring." This resulted in the publication of *A Book of Saints and Wonders Put Down Here by Lady Gregory According to the Old Writings and the Memory of the People of Ireland*, published by the Dun Emer Press in 1906 and the following year in London by Murray.

Already in 1900 Lady Gregory had plunged into the literary revival by editing *Ideals in Ireland* — a collection of essays which included *Nationality and Imperialism* by AE (G. W. Russell), *The Battle of Two Civilizations* by D. P. Moran, *Literature and the Irish Language* by George Moore (in which Moore, who did not himself speak Irish, compared the Irish language to a spring rising in the mountains, increasing into a rivulet and then becoming a great river), *What Ireland is Asking For* by Douglas Hyde, and *The Literary Movement in Ireland* by W. B. Yeats. Lady Gregory learned Irish as an adult from the people and at the beginning of the century she worked diligently in the National Library on translations. The combination of her studies and her firsthand folkloring is apparent in her plays, and it is on her achievement as a dramatist that her place in literature principally depends, but she also published the direct results of her researches. *Poets and Dreamers: Studies and translations from the Irish*, appeared in 1903; *Irish folk-history plays* came in two series, the tragedies in 1912, the tragic comedies in 1923; the first series of *Visions and Beliefs in the West of Ireland*, with two essays and notes by Yeats, was published in 1920, and her prose translations from the Irish were published as *The Kiltartan Poetry Book*.

Lady Gregory advertised her search for talent and helped many struggling writers, but she failed to detect James Joyce's genius; when he went to see her, she rebuffed him. Immediately after his unsuccessful interview, according to Gogarty, Joyce composed this limerick:

> There was a kind Lady called Gregory,
> Said, "Come to me poets in beggary"
> But found her imprudence
> When thousands of students
> Cried, "All we are in that catégory."

Gogarty saw the strained "catégory" as the beginning of Joyce's experimenting with words.

Believing that her sale of the Coole Park estate to the Land Commission and the Department of Forestry in 1927 would "give employment and be for the good and dignity of the country," Lady Gregory also hoped that the house would have a future, but it was demolished in 1941 and the library where she wrote her most famous play, *The Rising of the Moon*, has gone. The autographed beech tree where distinguished visitors carved their initials has survived, and in the spring, the bluebells, the anemones, the tufts of primroses, and the wild violets faintly recall the past beauty of the place which, fortunately, was immortalized by Yeats in his poem, *Coole Park, 1929*:

> I meditate upon a swallow's flight,
> Upon an aged woman and her house,
> A sycamore and lime-tree lost in night
> Although that western cloud is luminous,
> Great works constructed there in nature's spite
> For scholars and for poets after us,
> Thoughts long knitted into a single thought,
> A dance-like glory that those walls begot.
>
> There Hyde before he had beaten into prose
> That noble blade the Muses buckled on,
> There one that ruffled in a manly pose
> For all his timid heart, there that slow man,
> That meditative man, John Synge, and those
> Impetuous men, Shawe-Taylor and Hugh Lane
> Found pride established in humanity,
> A scene well set and excellent company.
>
> They came like swallows and like swallows went,
> And yet a woman's powerful character
> Could keep a swallow to its first intent;
> And half a dozen in formation there,
> That seemed to whirl upon a compass-point,
> Found certainty upon the dreaming air,
> The intellectual sweetness of those lines
> That cut through time or cross it withershins.
>
> Here, traveller, scholar, poet, take your stand
> When all those rooms and passages are gone,
> When nettles wave upon a shapeless mound
> And saplings root among the broken stone,
> And delicate—eyes bent upon the ground,
> Back turned upon the brightness of the sun
> And all the sensuality of the shade—
> A moment's memory to that laurelled head.

Coole Park inspired another of Yeats's poems, *The Wild Swans at Coole*:

> The trees are in their autumn beauty,
> The woodland paths are dry,
> Under the October twilight the water
> Mirrors a still sky;

Upon the brimming water among the stones
Are nine-and-fifty swans.

The nineteenth autumn has come upon me
Since I first made my count;
I saw, before I had well finished,
All suddenly mount
And scatter wheeling in great broken rings
Upon their clamorous wings.

I have looked upon those brilliant creatures,
And now my heart is sore.
All's changed since I, hearing at twilight,
The first time on this shore,
The bell-beat of their wings above my head,
Trod with a lighter tread.

Unwearied still, lover by lover,
They paddle in the cold
Companionable streams or climb the air;
Their hearts have not grown old;
Passion or conquest, wander where they will,
Attend upon them still.

But now they drift on the still water,
Mysterious, beautiful;
Among what rushes will they build,
By what lake's edge or pool
Delight men's eyes when I awake some day
To find they have flown away?

Yeats visited nearly every summer for twenty years as a guest of Lady Gregory at Coole Park and then, in 1916, he purchased for £35 a ruined medieval tower house of the Burkes, Ballylee Castle, only three miles away. It was at Ballylee that he wrote many of the poems in his collection *The Tower*. In the poem which gave the collection its title, the poet wrote of his Connacht castle:

I pace upon the battlements and stare
On the foundations of a house, or where
Tree, like a sooty finger, starts from the earth;
And send imagination forth
Under the day's declining beam, and call
Images and memories
From ruin or from ancient trees,
For I would ask a question of them all.

And in another verse he reminisced on its past:

Before that ruin came, for centuries,
Rough men-at-arms, cross-gartered to the knees
Or shod in iron, climbed the narrow stairs,
And certain men-at-arms there were
Whose images, in the Great Memory stored,
Come with loud cry and panting breast
To break upon a sleeper's rest
While their great wooden dice beat on the board.

In *My House*, a part of *Meditations in Time of Civil War*, in the collection, Yeats wrote affectionately of Ballylee:

An ancient bridge, and a more ancient tower,
A farmhouse that is sheltered by its wall,
An acre of stony ground,
Where the symbolic rose can break in flower,
Old ragged elms, old thorns innumerable,
The sound of the rain or sound
Of every wind that blows;
The stilted water-hen
Crossing stream again
Scared by the splashing of a dozen cows;

A winding stair, a chamber arched with stone,
A grey stone fireplace with an open hearth,
A candle and written page.
Il Penseroso's Platonist toiled on
In some like chamber, shadowing forth
How the daemonic rage
Imagined everything.
Benighted travellers
From markets and from fairs
Have seen his midnight candle glimmering.

Two men have founded here. A man-at-arms
Gathered a score of horse and spent his days
In this tumultuous spot,
Where through long wars and sudden night alarms
His dwindling score and he seemed castaways
Forgetting and forgot;
And I, that after me
My bodily heirs may find,
To exalt a lonely mind,
Befitting emblems of adversity.

But it was not only Coole Park and Ballylee in Connacht that inspired Yeats. One of his best-known poems, *The Lake Isle of Innisfree*, was written of the tiny wooded island in

Lough Gill which is on the border of Sligo and Leitrim:

> I will arise and go now, and go to Innisfree,
> And a small cabin build there, of clay and wattles made;
> Nine beanrows will I have there, a hive for the honeybee,
> And live alone in the bee-loud glade.
>
> And I shall have some peace there, for peace comes
>   dropping slow,
> Dropping from the veils of the morning to where the
>   cricket sings;
> There midnight's all a glimmer, and noon a purple glow,
> And evening full of the linnet's wings.
>
> I will arise and go now, for always night and day
> I hear lake water lapping with low sounds by the shore;
> While I stand on the roadway, or on the pavements gray,
> I hear it in the deep heart's core.

The southern shores of beautiful Lough Gill are flanked by high, wooded bluffs; Slish Wood is famous for its riot of ferns and mosses. A few miles away, north of Sligo, is Lissadell, the Grecian Revival mansion of the Gore-Booth family, once the home of Yeats's friends, the sisters Eva, a poetess, and Constance, who as Countess Markiewicz is remembered as a heroine of the Irish struggle for independence. In a poem written in 1927 Yeats recalled the sisters and their Connacht home:

> The light of evening, Lissadell,
> Great windows open to the south,
> Two girls in silk kimonos, both
> Beautiful, one a gazelle.
> But a raving autumn shears
> Blossom from the summer's wreath;
> The older is condemned to death,
> Pardoned, drags out lonely years
> Conspiring among the ignorant.
> I know not what the younger dreams—
> Some vague Utopia—and she seems,
> When withered old and skeleton-gaunt,
> An image of such politics.
> Many a time I think to seek
> One or the other out and speak
> Of that old Georgian mansion, mix
> Pictures of the mind, recall

> That table and the talk of youth,
> Two girls in silk kimonos, both
> Beautiful, one a gazelle.

In the last verse of a long poem, *Under Ben Bulben*, Yeats thought of his own death and his burial in the graveyard of Drumcliff:

> Under bare Ben Bulben's head
> In Drumcliff churchyard Yeats is laid.
> An ancestor was rector there
> Long years ago, a church stands near,
> By the road an ancient cross.
> No marble, no conventional phrase;
> On limestone quarried near the spot
> By his command these words are cut;
>
> > Cast a cold eye
> > On life, on death.
> > Horseman, pass by!

The region of Sligo which Yeats admired so much has become known as "the Yeats Country." One of his beloved places there was Dooney Rock at the foot of the Ox Mountains. From the top of this great forest-clad rock there is a sublime panorama of the gray limestone mountains of the Dartry Range, the massive prow of Ben Bulben, and, below, the Garavogue River, and the glittering silvery waters and wooded peninsulas of Lough Gill.

The inland counties of Leitrim and Roscommon are far less famous for scenic beauty than the seaboard counties but they have many lovely tranquil places which, just because they are less famous, are less trampled by the visitor. There is a joke about Leitrim, the lake-studded heart of the Ancient Kingdom of Breffni, which would have it that land in the county is sold not by the acre but by the gallon. Sean O'Faolain has described Leitrim as "a boggy, soggy, rushy land, full of burrowing streams, tiniest crevices of water everywhere." The physiognomy of Roscommon and Leitrim has changed radically since the Middle Ages when the Upper Shannon Valley was densely wooded, and when parties of Spaniards from the shipwrecked Armada struggled through the woods to find asylum. The urbane Captain de Cuellar, who left an account of his adventures, described the inhabitants of Leitrim as "savages," for they appeared to him so rough and backward. Some patches of the once vast forest of Coill Conchobhair which reached to the shores of Lough

Key survive in the former demesne of Rockingham, now a Forest Park. In this magnificent setting beneath the Curlew Mountains the Forestry Department is attempting to re-create the rich wooded landscape. In former times immense oak woods stretched westwards also from Lough Ree to the Connacht Uplands. Fasach-Coille, the great wood near Lough Allen, in County Leitrim, has also almost entirely vanished, the victim of iron mining in the region. The ironworks were moved from one wooded site to another until the charcoal supply was exhausted. Further man-made changes in the Leitrim landscape are to be expected with the renewed mining interest and speculation in the Arigna Valley area of County Leitrim.

A native of County Roscommon, Douglas Hyde was another scion of the Anglo-Irish Connacht gentry who espoused the Irish cause, but he diverged from most of Lady Gregory's group in aiming at a true revival of literature in the Irish language rather than a literary output of Irish inspiration in English. He was born in 1860 at Tibohine Rectory, Frenchpark, where his father was Rector; as a child, he was fascinated by the life, the lore, and the Irish language of the Connacht country where he grew up. Remarkable to him too was its contrast to the English-speaking anglophile world of his own family, related to the local landlord, Lord De Freyne, whose seat, French Park, an elegant Palladianesque mansion, stood in the center of an Irish-speaking district. Hyde, who learned Irish from the gamekeeper and local workmen, became such a zealous Irish speaker himself that when he took the oath in Latin to be admitted to the library of Trinity College, the Provost, Dr. Jellett, noticing his unusual pronunciation, asked him if he had learned his Latin on the Continent. When Hyde replied that he had not, he was further interrogated; when he explained that his pronunciation was based on the analogy of Latin with Irish, the Provost told him to leave the room.

In an early poem, Smaointe Bhróin, in the Dublin University Review, Hyde lamented the disappearance from their land of Irish people, due to emigration. The Irish language was dying fast in the second half of the last century and Hyde was passionately keen to remedy this and to shatter the indifference with which many people watched what was happening. In 1892, he delivered his now-famous lecture to the National Literary Society, entitled The Necessity for De-Anglicizing Ireland, at which he explained, "When we speak of de-anglicizing the Irish Nation we mean it, not as a protest against imitating what is best in the English people, for that would be absurd, but rather to show the folly of neglecting what is Irish and hastening to adopt pell-mell and indiscriminately everything that is English simply because it is English." In 1889, for his first published work, a collection of folk tales entitled Leabhar Sgeuluigheachta, Hyde adopted an Irish pseudonym, An Craoibhin Aoibhinn. In 1890 he published an English translation of some Irish tales as Beside the Fire and published them the following year in Irish as Cois na Teine. Of his considerable literary output, the most successful work was his Love Songs of Connacht in Irish accompanied with the English translations, published in 1893. One of these songs, which Hyde heard from a woman in County Roscommon, celebrates Nephin, a mountain in western Mayo. The soft, simple love song of a man, the English version begins:

> Did I stand on the bald top of Néfin
> And my hundred-times loved one with me,
> We should nestle together as safe in
> Its shade as the birds on a tree.

But none of these Connacht love songs evokes better the gentle communion of the people with nature and the land than If I Were to Go West, the translation of a sorrowful lament of a girl who has been crossed by her lover:

> If I were to go west, it is from the west I would not come,
> On the hill that was highest, 't is on it I would stand,
> It is the fragrant branch I would soonest pluck
> And it is my own love I would quickest follow.
>
> My heart is as black as a sloe,
> Or as a black coal that would be burnt in a forge,
> As the sole of a shoe upon white halls,
> And there is great melancholy over my laugh.
>
> My heart is bruised, broken,
> Like ice upon the top of water,
> As it were a cluster of nuts after their breaking,
> Or a young maiden after her marrying.
>
> My love is of the colour of the blackberries,
> And the colour of the raspberry on a fine sunny day.
> Of the colour of the darkest heath-berries of the
>   mountain,
> And often there has been a black head upon a bright
>   body.

Time it is for me to leave this town,
The stone is sharp in it, and the mould is cold;
It was in it I got a blame without riches
And a heavy word from the band who back-bite.

I denounce love; woe is she who gave it
To the son of you woman, who never understood it.
My heart in my middle, sure he has left it black,
And I do not see him on the street or in any place.

Hyde firmly believed that only in a nationwide revival of the Irish language and culture would the people of Ireland be able to make of the present a rational continuation of the past. He hoped also for a retrieval and revival of Irish music and musical instruments, and of the ancient Irish games and of old Connacht dances like the Waves of Tory and the Bridge of Athlone, as well as the language and literature, in order to generate a popular national cultural renaissance. To further this, Hyde and other enthusiasts founded the Gaelic League in 1893. The League was apolitical, but by its nature it was bound to attract people with nationalist tendencies. Hyde himself admitted, "it is our own Gaelic past which, though the Irish race does not recognize it, is really at the bottom of the Irish heart and prevents us becoming citizens of the Empire." Consequently, reviving the Gaelic past could be expected to accentuate the alienation of the Irish from Britain. The movement therefore had its enemies on both political and cultural grounds. One academic claimed that all the Irish texts were either religious, silly, or indecent. However, the Gaelic League was a success, and after Hyde's publicity tour through the United States from New York to San Francisco and back through Canada in 1905, branches were formed across the Atlantic. *Ceilidhthe*, evening entertainments of Irish dancing, songs, and recitation were sponsored by the League as well as Summer Colleges and other activities.

The new constitution of Ireland, marking a further stage of its independence, came into force on December 29, 1937, and in May, 1938, Hyde, who had already served as a Free State Senator, was called out of his rural retirement at Ratra House in his native Roscommon, having been elected without opposition the first President of Ireland.

Edward Martyn of Tullira Castle, County Galway, a neighbor and friend of Lady Gregory's, was another figure in the promotion of the arts. He was responsible for launching the first studio to make stained glass in Ireland, the influential and successful *An Tur Gloine*, under the direction

of the artist Sarah Purser. Martyn, a musical dilettante, was also, like Yeats and Moore, a director of the Irish Literary Theatre. He tried his hand as a dramatist too and was an early patron of Dublin's famous Abbey Theatre, whose foundation was discussed and planned in Connacht with Yeats and Lady Gregory at Durras House, the residence of Count Florimond de Basterot. Despite Edward Martyn's ardent Catholicism and his enthusiasm for the Irish arts, according to Lennox Robinson his own Galway country people never really warmed to him, although he had even supported Sinn Fein because, in Robinson's words, "he hated England with a real hatred."

Animosity to the English and to the big landowners had grown in intensity and reached a peak during the agrarian disturbances in the decades after the Famine. The incident of Captain Boycott, a land agent in County Mayo, gave the English language a new verb. Something of the current extremes in lack of comprehension, tact, and sympathy can be gauged from the rabidly anti-Irish memoirs of a Mrs. Houston, published in London in 1879, entitled *Twenty Years in the Wild West or Life in Connaught*. Mrs. Houston's attitude so incensed one reader of the copy of her work in the National Library of Ireland that he (or she) has written "you dirty old b......" under the author's name. Captain Houston and his wife, an intrepid and insensitive Englishwoman whose other literary endeavor was *A Yacht Voyage to Texas*, leased 70,000 acres in the mountains of Mayo at what she admitted was "a low rent." Recollecting later how she felt at the beginning of her Irish adventure she wrote, "The bitter and unquenchable hatred of the Celt towards the Saxon was, equally to us, an unknown evil. Only by slow degrees did the reality of this detestation come home to us. And sorely had we to rue a condition of things which no efforts on our part could overcome or even alleviate."

The "efforts" she made appear to have been provocative to say the least; had they been designed to invite the "unquenchable hatred of the Celt" toward her she could hardly have done better. As soon as she arrived in Mayo she plunged into the local election, striving, as she put it, "in a quiet way, to the best of my powers, but alas! entirely in vain, to snatch, if such a thing were possible, one vote at least from the grasping hands of the Roman Catholic party!" The Houstons' next "effort" was to import a number of Presbyterian shepherds and their families from Scotland to work on their estate. But things did not go well. The real adversary, Mrs. Houston knew, was the Catholic clergy who "spread disaffection ... encouraged drunkenness" and "from their altars ordered the ignorant and bigoted populace to kill, destroy and smash up." Her antipathy for the priests reached paroxysms of prejudice, snobbery and racism. To her they were "evil-looking, black-visaged men," and she was able to assert that "during all the years I passed in Ireland, I never remember to have seen a fair-complexioned priest." However, when Mrs. Houston met the Archbishop of Tuam she condescended to address him as "Your Grace," but not without reservations, because, as she put it, "he was not the cleanest old man I ever met"; worse still, he spoke with an Irish brogue. Fortunately there were not many landlords like the Houstons, but even so there were too many. Mrs. Houston's book, which the publisher thought would be informative to the public in England, may now be good for a few laughs, but just beneath the cant there is the subject for heartache, a raw view of agrarian misery in Connacht only one hundred years ago. The Irish language has some rich curses which the tenants of the Houstons' acres may well have invoked against these nineteenth-century adventurers. Perhaps they tried "*Croch ard gaoithe chuige*" (A high windy gallows to him), or "*Mallacht na mbaintreach agus na agalrach ort*" (The curse of the widows and orphans be upon you). Anyway, the Houstons packed and returned whence they came, their colonial effort a total failure.

Not only the settlers were bad landlords; Galway folklore tells of a cruel Irish landlord, one of the O'Flahertys, who not only evicted a poor widow on his estate in the winter but even sheared her last two sheep. The widow's dead son, who had been a priest, cursed O'Flaherty from beyond the grave. Within a month O'Flaherty died and then people saw his ghost pacing the shore of Lough Corrib, its legs as scrawny as the shanks of a shorn sheep. Widow's curses were considered particularly efficacious. A folk story from Lady Gregory's *Kiltartan* relates that a bad landlord there enclosed a well which the people had used time out of mind. The landlord apprehended a poor widow whom he caught trespassing on her way to the well to get water, and he gave her a beating. The widow fell to her knees, loosened her hair, and solemnly cursed the landlord. From that moment lameness came on him; he became crippled and then he died. A far less sympathetic Galway widow was Nuala Burke, known as "*Nuala na Mideoige*" (Nuala of the Dagger), because, according to the story, she murdered her twelve sons by stabbing them. When she was dying she dug her own grave under the walls of her island castle of Corlough and then lay in it. The walls of the castle collapsed and the stones covered her body.

Despite some obstinate and recalcitrant settlers like the Houstons, Connacht's strength in acculturating and hibernicizing incomers over the centuries has been remarkable. While in the other provinces the settlers often tended to impose their own style on the indigenous population, this was not generally the case in Connacht. The Anglo-Normans who managed to push into the Kingdom of Connacht were soon hibernicized, and in succeeding centuries identified their interests with those of the older Irish inhabitants to such a degree that today their very names seem as native as any. The de Burgos or Burkes, the most populous of the families of Norman origin, spread quickly through Galway and Mayo and some branches of their descendants adopted Irish patronyms for their family name — Mac Gibbon, Mac Nicholas, and Mac Philbin in County Mayo; Mac Davie, Jennings, and Mac Redmond in County Galway. Similarly some of the Stauntons became Mac Evilly, some of the Prendergasts became Mac Morris, a branch of the Barretts of Western Mayo became Mac Andrew, and the de Nagles adopted the name Mac Costelloe, now more frequently in use as Costello. The other important families of Norman origin in Connacht were the Dillons, mainly in County Roscommon, the Frenches, with widespread branches in the same county, the de Berminghams, and the Jordans. Two populous hibernicized Connacht families came from Wales — the Taaffes, in the thirteenth century, and the Joyces.

The Joyces and the Frenches were among the families of merchant princes who prospered in the port city of Galway. Twelve of the fourteen great families who were prominent there for centuries were hibernicized descendants of the invaders; two only were old Irish stock: the Kirwans, originally O'Kirwan, and the Norman-sounding Darcys, originally Ó Dorchaidhe. The fourteen families who were known as "The Tribes of Galway" accumulated fortunes in trade and extended their holdings to rural areas of Connacht. The most prominent were the de Lench family, who became Lynch, and the Blake family, descended from Richard Caddell, Sheriff of Connacht in 1303. The other "Tribes," besides these two and the four others already mentioned, were the families of Bodkin, Martin, Skerett, Browne, Athy, Deane, Fant, and Morris.

Of the ancient Irish families in Connacht, the most illustrious, of course, were the O'Conors, once Kings of Connacht, represented today in the male line by the O'Conor Don whose seat is Clonalis in County Roscommon. The MacDermots, once hereditary marshals of the O'Conors, had a territory in County Roscommon; their present representative is the Mac Dermot, Prince of Coolavin.

The princely family of O'Rourke were sovereigns of Breffni which embraced Leitrim; two other families of the county were branches of the O'Rourke clan, the Mac Goldricks and the Mac Murrows; the O'Curneens were the ollavs of the O'Rourkes. Other Leitrim septs were the Mac Weeneys who came in from Moy Lurg, the Mac Governs or Magaurans, the O'Gallons, the Mac Clancys of Rossclogher on Lough Melvin, the O'Meehans who originated in Munster, the Mac Gilhooleys who were a branch of the O'Mulveys, the Mac Ganlys or Mac Shanleys, the Mac Sharrys, and the Mac Rannalls often anglicized as Reynolds.

The most prominent old Irish families in Sligo were a branch of the royal O'Conors known as O'Conor Sligo; the O'Garas of Coolavin; the two branches of O'Haras—O'Hara Boy and O'Hara Reagh; the O'Dowds; the Mac Donaghs, who were a branch of the Mac Dermots, the O'Breslins, a brehon family; and a family of historians called Mac Firbis.

Kelly or O'Kelly is now the second most numerous surname in Ireland, surpassed only by Murphy. The most important O'Kelly sept originated in County Galway where many of its branches were prominent. The O'Flahertys, their subsept the Galway Mac Donaghs, their physicians the O'Canavans, and their ollavs the Mac Kilkellys were among the leading families in Iar Connacht. Other prominent families of County Galway besides the Burkes, the fourteen "Tribes of Galway," two septs named O'Divilly, and two named Mac Hugh, were the O'Maddens; the O'Shaughnessys in the Barony of Kiltartan who claimed descent from Daithi, the last pagan King of Ireland; the O'Dalys; the O'Donnellans; the O'Mullallys, often shortened to Lally; the O'Clerys of Kilmacduagh; the O'Flahertys; the O'Mulrooneys, often now corrupted to Moroney; the O'Fahys near Loughrea; and the O'Havertys near Craughwell. The Mac Nevin sept were poets and physicians in the county, the Mac Egans were brehons, and the O'Callinans were an erenagh family.

In Mayo besides the hibernicized Anglo-Norman families already mentioned, there was the illustrious old Irish family of O'Malley, one of the Irish names that rarely dropped the O' over the centuries. The O'Malleys were intrepid seamen. One of the daughters of this family in the reign of Elizabeth I, Grania or Grace O'Malley, gained fame for her daring maritime exploits and has gone down in popular history as "the Pirate Queen." The O'Fergus family were physicians to the O'Malleys. The Mac Gannons, the O'Cannys, and the

Mac Cunneens, a literary family, all belonged to Erris. The Mac Hales came from near Killala and the O'Moran sept in Mayo belonged near Ardnaree.

In the Cromwellian resettlement of Ireland in 1653, when areas of the country were allotted for various purposes, Leitrim was reserved for raising money to pay off the arrears of the English military. Roscommon, Mayo, and Galway, as well as the neighboring county of Clare, were set aside as places of forced residence for about two thousand Catholic landowners and their families and followers from the other provinces, who were forcibly dispossessed and transplanted to this "reservation" west of the Shannon. This act, while it did get some "undesirables" out of the way, strengthened the hard core of Connacht antipathy to the English authorities.

In Penal times a number of the old Connacht families managed to survive by devious means such as arranging for the eldest son of each generation to conform to the Established Church, while the rest of the family remained Roman Catholic. Because of the number of conformations of convenience, intermarriage between families of the two faiths was fairly frequent among the old Connacht gentry. An example of this sort of intermarriage may be found in the ancestry of the novelist George Moore. His great-great-grandfather, John Moore of Ashbrook, a Protestant, married about 1730 Jane Lynch Athy, the daughter of a Galway Catholic family. It is not known whether their son George Moore was brought up a Protestant or a Catholic but he passed as a Catholic in Spain, where he married Catherine Killikelly of an expatriate Galway Catholic family. There were descendants of the "Wild Geese," men who fled to the continent after the defeat of James II in 1690, living in Catholic countries abroad, often soldiers of fortune, but like a number of Irish expatriates in Spain, Mr. Moore was in business as a merchant. He imported kelp from Connacht to manufacture iodine, and exported wines to Galway. When he returned to Connacht with a considerable fortune he built Moore Hall in County Mayo. His son John, a Roman Catholic, married a bride from the Protestant aristocracy, Louisa Browne, of the family of Lord Sligo, and granddaughter of the first Earl of Altamont. Their son, the novelist's father, was brought up a Roman Catholic and married into the old Connacht Catholic gentry, to Mary Blake, whose forebears were among the "Tribes of Galway."

George Moore was born in 1852 at Moore Hall, a fine mansion on the shores of Lough Carra, which fell victim to the I.R.A. campaign of burning the residences of Free State Senators, because the novelist's brother Maurice was a

Senator. In February, 1923 fire was put to the house and the leaping flames were reflected in the tranquil lake until only a smoldering shell remained. Animosity and agrarian discontent may have incited this act as well, for George Moore admitted that his family had looked upon and treated their tenants like animals, although his radical grandfather had been appointed Provisional Governor of Connacht when the French under General Humbert landed in an attempted invasion in 1798.

Moore and his cousin Edward Martyn were among the visitors to Coole Park remembered by the poet Austin Clarke in the first lines of his *The Echo at Coole*:

I stood one day in the great Pleasure Garden
At Coole, where the catalpa blossoms—handing
Out pods in Autumn, long as cigars that George Moore
And Edward Martyn smoked after their dinner
At Tulira, Sad wilderness of panicles,
Roses gone thorning, seven leaves instead
Of five, gay, sportive blooms that had lost their seed
And names in lengthy Latin. I stared awhile
Beneath the copper beech where a railing guarded
Initials, wintered into the bark deep-cut,
Of W. B. and Y., A. G., A. J.
AE, and S. O'C.: thinking again
How Lady Gregory would drive twelve miles
Day after day, sun-reining in a phaeton, along
Her avenues—with Phaeton—through the Seven Woods,
By alleys of wild privet, lake-lingering,
To count the Swans for Willie.

When Moore died in London his ashes were sent back to Ireland. Oliver St. John Gogarty in silk hat and frock coat offered to row the funeral party across Lough Carra to Castle Island in the lake where the ashes were to be buried in sight of the ruins of Moore Hall. Gogarty, who found the task of rowing more strenuous than he had expected, shed some of his clothes, piece by piece. George Moore's sister, feigning alarm, remarked drily that she presumed Gogarty would retain his braces. On a more serious note, AE, one of the party, said in his funeral oration, "If his ashes have any sentience they will feel at home here, for the colours of Carra Lake remained in his memory when many of his other affections had passed." In Moore's *Evelyn Innes*, of 1898, the heroine and her lover, the young pantheistic musician Ulick, go to Ireland and make a pilgrimage on bicycles to the sacred places of the ancient pagan inhabitants. Like Augusta Gregory, Moore did love the land of Connacht although he did not share her love for the people. Lough Carra was the setting of his novel *The Lake*, published in 1905, but its prose bears no resemblance to that of the contemporary writers in Ireland and its theme reflected some of his passionate rejection of his cradle faith, Roman Catholicism. To the main character, an unhappy priest, Moore naughtily gave the name Oliver Gogarty. Moore wished to disassociate himself from the Catholics in Ireland and, in religion, what he called "the soft, peaty stuff that comes from Connaught." He argued that in Ireland, where the distinction embraced so much more than religion, one could only reject Catholicism by becoming a Protestant, as one had to be one or the other, and so he decided to be received into the Church of Ireland.

Moore collaborated with Yeats on the play *Diarmuid and Grania* in 1901. His collection of short stories, *The Untilled Field*, a portrait of Ireland, was first published in Irish as *An T-ur-Gort, Sgealtan* in 1902 and then in English the following year. Even later works have an Irish background, like his *Ulick and Soracha*, of 1926, written after Moore's disenchantment with the Irish Revival. While he was still enthusiastic about spoken Irish, Moore took some lessons but admitted that he was too old to learn the language. However, he was keen that his little nephews should speak and think in Irish. In a speech to the Irish Literary Society he said that he would arrange for them to have a nurse from the Aran Islands, and in the summer of 1900 wrote to his sister-in-law telling her that he would pay for this, and mentioned also that Hyde had informed him that very good Irish was spoken in the region about Moore Hall. The Irish-speaking nurse was a failure, so was the local Mayo schoolmaster, and Evelyn Moore reported that the other local Irish speakers were too dirty to let into the house. Moore, furious at what he considered his sister-in-law's lack of effort in ensuring that the children spoke Irish, wrote her in the spring of 1901 that "whether the nurses are dirty or ill-mannered are matters of no moment whatever," and that he had revoked his will, cutting out his nephews altogether unless they spoke Irish fluently within a year.

Moore's plan to bring a nurse from Aran is not surprising because Aran was a byword among the Celtic Revival enthusiasts. Yeats claimed that when he first met the young J. M. Synge in Paris he had advised him, "Go to the Aran Islands. Live there as if you were one of the people themselves: express a life that has never found expression." Whether because of Yeats's advice or not, Synge, a Dubliner who had studied Irish at Trinity and Celtic Civilization at the Sorbonne in Paris, went to Aran in 1898. He made his name with his plays based on stories he heard over the years on Inishmore and Inishmaan, two of the three humps of a limestone reef off Galway Bay that are the Aran Islands. They are still an individualistic Irish-speaking outpost of the industrial world. Electricity has not yet come to the islands, but there have been many changes since Synge described Aran, the spartan life of the islanders, and the traditional folk culture in his *The Aran Islands*, published in 1907. Not least of these changes are a lifeboat service which serves also as a sea ambulance, and a transportation link with the mainland by air. Today, the inhabitants, just under 1,000 on Inishmore, and between 300 and 400 each on Inishmaan and Inisheer, after weathering years of hardship are more concerned with economic than cultural development.

Synge described Kilronan, the harbor of Inishmore, as "the bay full of green delirium," and so it can often be when the weather is blustery and the sea is rough. Saint Enda, son of a King of Oriel, landed at Aran from the coast of Clare about 483 and founded a monastery which gained such a reputation as a novitiate and retreat that Aran was called "Aran of the Saints"; it is recorded that most of the famous founders of Early Christian monasteries in Ireland spent some time there, among them Saint Finnian of Clonard, Saint Finnian of Moville, Saint Kieran, Saint Kevin, Saint Colman, Saint Columcille, and Saint Carthage. Tradition has it that Saint Brendan the Navigator also came to Aran for Saint Enda's blessing before setting off on his transatlantic voyage. There are, not surprisingly, numerous Early Christian ruins on the islands, churches, towers, crosses, graves, cenotaphs, monastic cells, and holy wells. The dedications of the churches of Aran are like a litany of Irish saints: Saint Benen, Saint Kieran, Saint Soorney, Saint Brecan, Saint Enda, Saint Colman (Mac Duagh); each has a church on Inishmore. The Church of the Saints and the Church of the Four Comely Persons are also early stone edifices on the island; on Inisheer are the early churches of Saint Gobnet and of Saint Keevan, and on Inishmaan those of Kilcanonagh and of the Seven Sons of Kings. For most visitors, however, these interesting little monuments are upstaged by Dun Aengus, the magnificent stone fort that perches dramatically on the steep, sheer cliffs of Inishmore, surrounded by thousands of chevaux-de-frise, jagged stone stakes set to protect the fort from attack on the landward side.

During his sojourns in Aran, Synge observed the people and their customs. Their sense of nearness to death and their familiarity with the treachery of the sea is portrayed in his one-act masterpiece, *Riders to the Sea* (1904), set in "An island off the West of Ireland." Although he placed the action in "a lonely mountainous district in the east of Ireland," the play *The Well of the Saints* (1905) was inspired by a story told to Synge by an old man at the well beside the medieval *Teampul an Cheathrair Aluinn*, the church of the Four Comely Persons. In his preface to *The Playboy of the Western World* (1907), set "on a wild coast of Mayo," the playwright acknowledged his debt to the folk imagination of simple people he had met all along the west coast. A native Aran writer, Liam O'Flaherty, who came after Synge, has left poignant word pictures of life on the islands in his books, *The Wounded Cormorant* and *Going into Exile*, while Robert Flaherty's classic film, *Man of Aran*, gave a dramatic visual account of island life, portrayed with some artistic license.

In Synge's time many people insisted that the Aran islanders were pure ancient Irish stock, but the findings of experts who have made anthropological surveys and blood tests of the inhabitants indicate that they are of mixed ancestry. Their blood group frequencies differ from those of the inhabitants of the adjacent mainland but are similar to those found in the north of England and in the east of Ireland. That newcomers came in waves to Aran is clear from the fact that between the census of 1821 and a survey of 1892, no less than seventeen new family surnames appeared on the islands, and a further twenty came in between 1892 and 1951. At the end of the sixteenth century when the O'Flahertys of Iar Connacht attempted to oust from Aran a branch of the O'Briens, the latter complained to Queen Elizabeth I, claiming that they had held the islands "time out of mind." The Crown decided the issue against both parties and attributed the islands to the Queen herself, who in turn granted them to an adventurer, Sir John Rawson, on condition that he maintain a garrison there of twenty English foot soldiers. Then in 1653 Cromwell was obliged to land a force of thirteen hundred men on Inishmore to take the islands. It appears that over the years the soldiers of the garrison intermarried with the old island stock and with incomers from the mainland; but as elsewhere in Connacht the old language, culture, and customs were dominant. The appearance of the English surname Wiggins as one of the island family surnames in 1821 supports the theory of descent from some of the English garrison, unless it is derived from MacGuigan, which is unlikely.

The commonest island surnames now are Faherty or O'Faherty, and O'Flaherty (both originally septs from the mainland of Galway), Conneely, Hernon, and Dirrane.

On Inishmaan especially, the ancient language flourishes, although many of the old customs are spent. It is still possible on Aran to share some of Synge's experiences, to sit alone on the cliffs by Dun Aengus and watch the gannets far below as they swoop for mackerel, to hear in the little houses, as he did, "a continual drone of Gaelic coming from the kitchen," to ride the waves in a curragh, "moving away from civilization in this rude canvas canoe of a model that has served primitive races since men first went to sea," or to wander on the cliffs in the wind until one's hair is stiff with salt. Keening, the ancient mourning wail which Synge called "the profound ecstasy of grief", is heard no more and the storytellers who delighted him have died away. But on a clear evening the sun still stands like an aureole behind Inishmaan, and across Galway Bay in the luminescent Atlantic light the Twelve Pins of Connemara are tinged with mauve and shades of scarlet, and as Maurya says at the end of *Riders to the Sea*, "What more can we want than that? No man at all can be living forever, and we must be satisfied."

Hawthorn or whitethorn, known popularly as May because its white flowers blossom in that month, Ballyhaunis, County Roscommon.

above: *Rockfleet Castle, County Mayo. This tower house on an inlet of Clew Bay was once a residence of Granuaile or Grace O'Malley, known as "the Pirate Queen." She beat off an English seaborne attack against the castle, but later she appeared before Elizabeth I and was granted permission to attack the queen's enemies.*

left: *Dungory Castle, Kinvara Bay, County Galway, built in the sixteenth century by an O'Heyne chief but passed later to the Burke and Martyn families. It was first repaired and restored by Edward Martyn of Tullira, and then acquired by Oliver St. John Gogarty, so that he could have a place near the Kiltartan "letterati" in Lady Gregory's circle.*

right: *Ben Bulben, in the heart of "Yeats Country," County Sligo, is not a mountain but the scarped edge of a limestone plateau, described by Yeats as the "cold and vapour-turbaned steep." Alpine saxifrage, green spleenwort, mountain avens, and cushion pink thrive on the calcareous cliffs.*

below: *A cow grazes near Clifden, Connemara, County Galway. In the foreground, a bank of montbretia, an African garden hybrid, which has become naturalized in parts of Ireland.*

following spread: *Looking across the lake at Loughrea, County Galway.*

opposite: *A pious local tradition attributes supernatural powers to the spring known as St. Brendan's Well, Carrowbeg, County Mayo, on the shore of Clew Bay. Such holy places were frequently chosen as burial grounds.*

below: *The carved brown sandstone doorway of the twelfth-century cathedral at Clonfert, County Galway, the supreme achievement of Irish-Romanesque decoration.*

Making Hay. opposite: *A farmer brings in the hay, Inishmore, Aran Islands. In the last decade a few motorized vehicles have been introduced;* below: *Near Killary Bay, County Galway, a farmer has prudently covered his haycocks with protective netting.*

above: *On the roadside near Eyrecourt, County Galway, along a favorite Tinker circuit, travelers have left their dog to guard their cart.*

right: *Mr. Moran's unchanged old farmhouse, with byre attached, near Carrowbeg, County Mayo, would have been a distinctly superior farm dwelling in the last century. In 1861, three and a half million of Ireland's total population of four and a half million lived in mud cabins, and over one million families shared a one-room dwelling.*

left: *The statue of Saint Patrick at the base of Croagh Patrick, where the pilgrims' arduous trail begins.*

right: *The gleaming white trail to the summit of Croagh Patrick, County Mayo, is trod annually by thousands of devout pilgrims.*

above: *The medieval doorway of Clontuskert Abbey, County Galway, was built in 1471. The figures above the door represent Saint Michael the Archangel (with a sword and scales for weighing souls), Saint John the Baptist, Saint Catherine, and a bishop.*

opposite: *Part of the once-busy quay, Westport, County Mayo.*

following spread: *The bedroom of Thoor Ballylee, County Galway. The poet W.B. Yeats purchased this sixteenth-century tower house for £35 in 1916; although Yeats lived here only intermittently, he often wrote of the tower and called it "this blessed place."*

top: *Children of a traveling family (Tinkers) in front of the ruins of Roscommon Castle.*

bottom : *Donkey cart with car wheels at Carrowmore, County Mayo.*

opposite: *Cows going to be milked, County Mayo.*

above: *Lads at Gort, County Galway, rest from their bicycling before the nineteenth-century window of a sweet shop.*

right: *"High Class Restaurant," Ballinasloe, County Galway.*

above: *Castle Island, Lough Carra, County Mayo. Lough Carra remained in the memory of the novelist George Moore after many other affections had passed. When he died, Oliver St. John Gogarty rowed the funeral party across these waters to bury Moore's ashes on Castle Island, in sight of Moore's family home, Moore Hall.*

opposite: *From Leenane to Renvyle in County Galway, the road passes Lough Fee.*

opposite: *Donkeys on the Corraun Peninsula, County Mayo.*

above: *Mallarany, Clew Bay, County Mayo. In this region, heaths of* Erica mediterranea, *an exotic heather that reached Ireland from the Iberian peninsula in post-glacial times, shelter from the ocean winds.*

below: *Connemara ponies, beside Derryclare Lough, County Galway. Hardy, sure-footed, and docile, this native breed is used for riding and show-jumping.*

opposite: *Lichen–covered granite boulders at Roundstone, County Galway.*

below: *The boat slip, Mallarany, Clew Bay, County Mayo.*

following spread: *Dooega Head on the western coast of Achill Island, County Mayo.*

above: *Autumn, near Bangor Erris in the far west of County Mayo.*

opposite: *Lough Talt, County Sligo.*

left: *Dun Aengus, Inishmore, Aran Islands, the most spectacular stone fort in Western Europe, dates from the Iron Age.*

right: *Temple Benen, Inishmore, Aran Islands, a fine example of an Early Christian single-cell church, built of stone, with a steeply-pitched roof.*

top left and right: *The cliffs of Inishmore, the largest of the Aran Islands.*

below left: Armeria maritima, *known as thrift or sea pink, is common on the cliffs near the sea in Ireland, leaving soft springy cushions after the bright pink flowers have gone.*

Houses on Inishmore, Aran Islands.

further Reading

Ancient Monuments of Northern Ireland, vols. I and II. Belfast: Her Majesty's Stationery Office, 1975.

De Breffny, Brian. *Castles of Ireland*. London: Thames and Hudson, 1977.

De Breffny, Brian, ed. *The Irish World*. New York: Harry N. Abrams, Inc., 1977.

De Breffny, Brian and Ffolliott, Rosemary. *The Houses of Ireland: Domestic Architecture from the 12th Century to the Edwardian Age*. New York: The Viking Press, 1975.

De Breffny, Brian and Mott, George. *The Churches and Abbeys of Ireland*. New York: W.W. Norton & Co., Inc., 1976.

Craig, M. *The Personality of Leinster*. Cork: The Mercier Press, Ltd., 1971.

Craig, M. and Glin, The Knight of. *Ireland Observed: A Guide to the Antiquities and Buildings of Ireland*. Cork: The Mercier Press, Ltd., 1970.

Evans, Emyr Estyn. *Irish Heritage*. Dundalk: Dundalgan Press, Ltd., 1942. Chester Springs: Dufour Editions, Inc., 1950.

———— *The Personality of Ireland*. Cambridge: The Cambridge University Press, 1973.

———— *Mourne Country: Landscape and Life in South Down*. Dundalk: Dundalgan Press, Ltd., 1967.

Flower, R. *The Irish Tradition*. Oxford: The Oxford University Press, 1947.

Gibbings, R. *Sweet Cork of Thee*. New York: E.P. Dutton, 1952.

Guinness, Desmond and Ryan, William. *Irish Houses and Castles*. New York: The Viking Press, 1971.

Hall, Mr. and Mrs. S. C. *Ireland, Its Scenery and Character*, 3 vols. London: 1846.

Harbison, Peter. *The Archaeology of Ireland*. New York: Charles Scribner's Sons, 1976.

Harbison, Peter. *Guide to the National Monuments of Ireland*. New York: Irish Book Center, 1975.

Hayward, R. and Piper, Raymond. *Munster and the City of Cork*. London: Dent & Sons, Ltd., 1964.

Herity, Michael and Eogan, George. *Ireland in Prehistory*. Boston: Routledge and Kegan Paul, 1976.

Hill, Lord George. *Facts from Gweedore*. Belfast: Queen's University of Belfast, Institute of Irish Studies, 1972.

Lewis, Samuel. *A Topographical Dictionary of Ireland*, 2 vols. and atlas. Port Washington: Kennikat Press, 1970.

Malins, Edward and Glin, The Knight of. *Lost Demesnes*. London: Barrie & Jenkins, 1976.

Mason, T.H. *The Islands of Ireland*. Cork: The Mercier Press, Ltd., 1967.

Mitchell, F. *The Irish Landscape*. London: Collins Sons & Co., Ltd., 1977.

Morton, H.V. *In Search of Ireland*. London: Methuen & Co., Ltd., 1969.

Mould, Pochin, D.D.C. *Ireland from the Air*. Newton Abbot: David & Charles, Ltd., 1972.

O'Connor, F. *Leinster, Munster and Connaught*. London: n.d.

Praeger, R.L. *The Way That I Went*. Dublin: Figgis & Co., Ltd., 1969.

Rothery, S. *The Shops of Ireland*. Dublin: 1978.

Webb, D.A. *An Irish Flora*. Dundalk: Dundalgan Press, Ltd., 1943.

White, T. de Vere. *Leinster*. London: Faber & Faber, Ltd., 1968.

Whittow, J.B. *Geology and Scenery in Ireland*. London: Penguin Books, Ltd., 1974.

Wilde, Sir W. R. W. *Beauties of the Boyne and Blackwater*. Dublin: 1849.

Wilde, Sir W. R. W. *Lough Corrib*. Dublin: 1872.

Young, Arthur. *A Tour in Ireland*. Dublin: Irish University Press, 1970.

The cliffs of Inishmore, Aran Islands.

Chronology

SIXTEENTH CENTURY A.D.

1536	King Henry VIII declared supreme head on earth of the Church of Ireland. Reformation introduced; suppression of monasteries commenced
1541–43	Policy of surrender and re-grant introduced
1542	Lordship of Ireland ends. Henry VIII becomes King of Ireland
1556	Plantation of Leix and Offaly
1567	Battle of Farsetmore; O'Neill defeated and his rebellion in Ulster ended
1569–73	First Desmond Rebellion in Munster
1571–75	Attempts at colonization in Ulster
1579–83	Second Desmond Rebellion in Munster
1585	Composition of Connacht formalized
1580	Papal expeditionary force lands in Kerry; all slain
1586	Confiscation of Desmond territory. Plantation of Munster begins
1594	Open rebellion in Ulster. The Nine Years War begins
1598	Insurrection

SEVENTEENTH CENTURY A.D.

1601	Battle of Kinsale; English victorious over Spaniards and Irish
1603	O'Neill surrenders. Treaty of Mellifont
1605	Plantation of Down and Antrim begun
1609	Articles of Plantation of Ulster issued. Colonization of Armagh, Coleraine (later Londonderry), Donegal, Cavan, Fermanagh, and Tyrone
1610–20	Minor plantations in Wexford, Longford, and Leitrim
1615	Composition of Connacht effected
1641	Insurrection in Ulster spreads throughout Ireland
1642	Rebels set up Provisional Government at Kilkenny as the Confederate Catholics of Ireland
1642–52	Civil war in Ireland
1649	Cromwell lands in Ireland, takes Drogheda and engages in campaign to subdue Ireland
1653	Cromwellian conquest accomplished. Irish landowners transplanted; massive confiscations and redistribution of land to Protestant settlers
1660	Restoration of the monarchy; Charles II
1662–65	Acts of Settlement and Explanation
1689	James II lands at Kinsale
1690	William III lands at Carrickfergus. War of the Two Kings. Battle of the Boyne; William III victorious
1691	Battle of Aughrim; siege and surrender of Limerick; victory of William III; Treaty of Limerick. Ten thousand or more Jacobite Irish go into exile on the continent; their estates are confiscated
1698	Roman Catholic hierarchy ordered to leave Ireland and Regulars of all orders expelled

EIGHTEENTH CENTURY A.D.

1702–15	Promulgation of Penal Laws
1720	Phase of country house building begins, increasing through the century; accompanied by development of towns and estate villages and intensive building in Dublin
1778	Catholic Relief Bill
1782	Irish Parliament declared independent
1791	Society of United Irishmen founded
1795	Orange Order founded to combat Defenderism and Popery

| 1796 | French fleet sails into Bantry Bay |
| 1798 | Rebellion breaks out mainly in Ulster and in County Wexford. French land at Killala Bay, County Mayo, with 1,000 troops; forced to surrender. Another French expedition foiled; ships captured off coast of Donegal |

NINETEENTH CENTURY A.D.

1801	Dublin Parliament abolished. Ireland united with Great Britain to form United Kingdom of Great Britain and Ireland
1810–23	Extensive Protestant church building in simplified Gothic style financed by the government through the Board of First Fruits
1823	The Catholic Association organized
1829	Roman Catholic emancipation act passed
1840	Young Ireland Party formed. Growth of nationalist feeling and a nationally oriented revival in literature and the arts emerges
1846	Failure of the potato crop. Famine, followed by massive emigration
1848	Encumbered Estates Act passed. Insurrection led by William Smith O'Brien fails
1858	Fenian Brotherhood and Irish Republican Brotherhood founded
1865–67	Fenian agitation
1869	Disestablishment of the Church of Ireland
1870	Landlord and Tenant Act passed. Home Government Association formed (later called Home Rule League)
1878	Land League founded
1880	Boycott incident in County Mayo
1881	Irish Land Law Act passed; Land Court and Land Commission established. Land League suppressed
1882	Phoenix Park murders
1891	Congested Districts Board established and Purchase of Land Act passed
1893	Gaelic League founded

TWENTIETH CENTURY A.D.

1903	Wyndham Act passed; as a consequence, a quarter of a million tenant farmers purchased their holdings
1909	Birrell Act passed. An additional 65,000 tenant farmers purchased their land
1913	Ulster Volunteer Force and Irish Volunteers founded
1914	Irish Home Rule Bill passed but suspended for the duration of World War I
1916	Easter Rising rebellion led by Irish Republican Brotherhood, Irish Volunteers, and Irish Citizen Army quelled; the leaders executed
1918–21	Guerrilla warfare
1919	Independent Dail set up in Dublin
1921	Inauguration of Northern Ireland Parliament. Anglo-Irish Treaty signed approving an Irish Free State with Dominion status
1922	Approval of treaty by Dail followed by outbreak of civil war between Free State and anti-Treaty factions. Irish Free State created
1923	Ceasefire agreement ends civil war
1937	New constitution; Republic of Ireland established with a president as head of state
1949	Republic of Ireland secedes from the British Commonwealth. Ireland Act passed in British Parliament
1967	Northern Ireland Civil Rights Association founded
1969	New phase of violence erupts in Northern Ireland; beginning of escalating guerrilla activity and involvement of British troops. Irish Republican Army (IRA) splits into left nationalist (Official) and right nationalist (Provisional) movements
1972	Dissolution of Northern Ireland Parliament; Direct Rule from Westminster established
1973	Republic of Ireland enters European Economic Community

Index

Illustrations are in *italics*. Color illustrations are further indicated by asterisks (*)